TARNISHED IN TINSELTOWN

A Medium for Revenge

EVA STOKES

PublishAmerica
Baltimore

This is a work of fiction. Names, characters, corporations, institutions, organizations, events or locales in this novel are either the product of the author's imagination or, if real, used fictitiously. Any resemblance to actual persons (living or dead) is entirely coincidental.

First printing

ISBN: 1-4241-3666-0
PUBLISHED BY PUBLISHAMERICA, LLLP
www.publishamerica.com
Baltimore

Printed in the United States of America

Dedication

For my sweet Habu, Forrest Walker,
whom I have "entertained to the last straw."

Acknowledgments

My heartfelt thanks to Jim Baumli, who made this book possible, and came up with the title. The two "Clothildes," Nika Halsey-Solomon and Kim Medeiros, who know what its like. Paula Kreuger, Andrea French, and Liz Anema for laughing so hard and making intelligent suggestions. Matthew McQueary, for loving me unconditionally through this process.

Everybody at PublishAmerica, especially Danielle and Rosemary, for giving me the opportunity and granting frequent requests for more time.

I also thank Captain Stoye Milburn of Satori, Captain Clemens Oestreich of Yacht Infinity, and the Infinity Rock Orchestra, especially Deepak Ramaprian and Kim Panzer. Thanks to everyone who has bought my albums, listened to my stories, gotten me drunk, gotten me sober, given me jewels, and fed me cheesecake.

TABLE OF CONTENTS

THE LAST EXORCIST
IN ENGLAND

I am living proof that it is still possible to have grand adventures in this world, if you have the courage to defy convention, incur the wrath of loved ones, and can put up with being treated like some kind of exotic pet in the name of anthropological interest.

I have seen the world from the backs of camels and elephants, traveled in rickshaws and private planes, sailed the seas in ancient hand-carved fishing boats and playboy yachts.

I have lived in jungles, caves and castles, and dined on everything from amphibious mud creatures to the delicately spiced tongues of rare North European songbirds.

I have survived pestilence, earthquake, and devastating storm, and have been the mistress of princes, friend of kings.

So if you bought all that, now I will describe the admittedly fishy-sounding events that led me to Hollywood and finally to here, an oasis in the middle of the desert, where my only companions are some endangered pupfish, a couple of frilly lizards, and the occasional oriental tourist.

England was not an easy place to live in the dark days of the late eighties.

Neighboring countries like France and Holland were almost modern back then, with drinkable tap water and central heating. Some countries even had actual fashion designers.

London's water was so filthy the European Council threatened to ban England from the planet if they didn't do something about it. The upper classes were bathing in clear bubbling Perrier and drinking champagne while the rest of the population chafed with ugly rashes and drank warm beer. Tourists could not be persuaded to stay long, despite enticing brass rubbing opportunities and chances to see the Queen's coronation crown.

The only identifiably English attempt at fashion (besides survival gear such as the Wellington boot and London Fog overcoat) was the discarded rags of obsolete chimney sweeps that were sold to punk rockers on Carnaby Street.

In those days England had a terrible, almost arctic climate and hardly anybody had central heating. Residential electricity was on a meter that cost fifty pence, like, every half hour. You had to keep lots of change handy or you'd spend an awful lot of time feeling your way around in the dark.

This was hell on the carpet during a party.

Since architecturally nothing had changed in about two thousand years, every dwelling had several fireplaces, but it was illegal to use them to keep warm because the city was still so polluted from the coal fumes that had killed off most of the plague survivors. Every winter thousands of old people and babies froze to death. There were tabloid rumors of a government plot to trim the elderly and newborns (typically those who require the most medical attention) from the population so that doctors, who tended to be of the ruling class, could spend more of their time fooling around in Scotland.

No matter the time or season London was always dark and stormy. It never stopped raining for more than three minutes and only a small percentage of the population could afford a car, so most people went from place to place carrying their stuff in plastic bags from the grocer.

Every household had a collection of umbrellas in the front hall, which I thought was a charmingly quaint archaic tradition. They were like, "We're British! We eat seven hundred-year-old fruitcake at Christmas and have a lot of umbrellas in our hall!" because God knows umbrellas were useless in the gale force winds that blew them inside out and also made hairdressing the country's least popular profession.

Since the famous London Fog overcoat was so expensive only members of the upper class could afford one, people ran around wearing about fifteen steaming sweaters with their hair blown every which way, aggressively wielding the dagger sharp skeleton of an erstwhile umbrella.

Not wishing to offend my xenophobic hosts I learned to do the same, and this is how I observed that the only way to tell the real homeless from everyone else was that they thanked you when you offered them money.

Of course, everybody got around by underground train, but above ground the preferred method of transport was running down the street. People were always running down the street because the bus was usually so late it came early, and I think in all the years I lived in London only three people actually managed to catch it, a feat that got their names in the newspapers and a lifetime of free pints at Ye Olde Slug & Lettuce.

London is quite different these days, I understand, what with that new Ferris wheel sculpture they put up by the Thames and Parliament renting some sunlight from Europe for the tourist season. I think someone told me they even have a decent restaurant now.

So, the way I ended up living in London was this: When I was fifteen I ran away from home to join a rock band and I really did wind up traveling all over the world by the time I was twenty. And I really did live in a castle, too, all right? People do, you know.

Anyway, jet-setting around with the aristocracy is a lot of fun, but at some point you've got to stop somewhere and try to be a little more serious. So when my blue-blooded boyfriend's mother forced him to dump me and marry a decent girl, I had to make a decision.

As much as I adore Paris I didn't want to do French pop music (if you've never heard any, get some; you've never laughed so hard in your life).

I tried, but it's really impossible to sing anything but drinking songs in German, and there wasn't any discernible music business in any other European country that I could find. I didn't want to return to America, so that left England, where I settled in as best I could, learned the lingo and habits of the natives, got a record deal, and I was soon busy making my own records and performing, as well as singing back-up with a number of refreshingly fearless English artists, creative people who wrote songs with wonderfully quirky lyrics and clever, interesting melodies. Yes, I am one of the fortunate few who remember when original music really was original, not a bland, predictable copy of something else!

Okay, back to the story.

One day a friend of mine called.

"Evie, will you do me a favor?"

"Sure!" I said.

"Well, you know my sister's boyfriend, Crispo, the heavy metal guitarist?"

"Yes."

"Crispo is trying to get a solo deal and needs a second back-up singer for a showcase in a couple of weeks, and I thought of you."

"Why, thank you!"

"He's on the dole so he can't pay," said my friend, "and I'm sure it will be quite hideous, but after all, weren't you in a heavy metal band before?"

"Who is the other singer?" I asked. "Do I know her?"

"I'm not sure. I think her name is Aura Jane."

"No, I don't know her. Well, I'm kind of busy, but I'll do it for you, okay?"

"Oh, thank you!"

I bundled up in my twelve sweaters, grabbed my umbrella, and off I ran to the audition.

Well, we never really know where fate will lead us next. Life is strange that way. If you're really paying attention you can kind of see where you're headed, in a general kind of way (The Bible describes it nicely as "seeing through a glass darkly"). But when you look back on things, it's perfectly obvious where you screwed up.

You hear people complaining about it all the time.

"That's when I decided to marry Ralph instead of making the quilt. Oh, if only I had made the quilt!" or "I moight still have moi leg if I'd gone on 'oliday to a place where there isn't any sharks, instead of that Hawaii!"

So when I realized Aura Jane had a little problem with some demons, I could have just walked away.

I could have got on the train and gone home.

I didn't *have* to get involved.

I didn't *have* to track down the last living exorcist in England, thereby acquiring primo crackpot status on three continents.

But that is what I did.

The Queenshagger audition took place in the appalling flat of the even more objectionable lead singer, Crispo, in a particularly nasty part of the city that is kept hidden from the eyes of the annual three or four hopelessly clueless tourists, at whom I always wanted to yell, "What's wrong with you? Why aren't you in Greece or Mexico?!"

Anyway.

I know something about heavy metal, so I can tell you that heavy metal bands are hideous on purpose. The success of the heavy metal band is entirely due to their appeal to suicidal addict types who have lost their jobs, spouses, and best friends because they are unable to master the confusion of living, which encompasses about 92.8% of the population of the Western Hemisphere at any given time.

In addition, a heavy metal concert is one of the only places where it is legal to trample strangers underfoot while screaming like a banshee, which is quite a cathartic experience. By the end of the concert whatever was bothering you doesn't seem so bad compared to the physical pain in your body, a distraction which can last for days if the concert was sufficiently violent.

If you look at history, man has always needed an outlet for his aggression, and the heavy metal concert is a logical evolutionary step due to the development of technology. The Gladiator Arena has given way to the Mosh Pit.

This is why heavy metal is successful. They are providing therapy for the masses whose lives have been rendered meaningless by mediocrity!

The problem with Crispo and Queenshagger was that they were hideous by accident, which was immediately apparent when I heard their first song. The screaming and posturing of the front man was typical, but the content of his rant was not that of a depressed but mother-loving good old boy from New Jersey or Stoke-on-Trent. This stuff was clearly written by an emotionally malformed deviant who had dwelt too long in the darkness of some damp underground chamber.

For example, one song's catchy little chorus went, "Makeup queen, so obscene…you've got too much (scream) *MAKEUP!* on!"

What is he talking about? Heavy metal guys love makeup! I decided Crispo must be a closet transvestite and was referring to something his mother once said to *him*.

Another one went, "You'll go to hell…you'll burn in hell…you ate the last piece of (screaming) *Coconut, coconut PIE!*"

Besides being a terrible lyric, this is way too personal a torment to have mass appeal. Who cares if he missed dessert?

Instead of the heroin-pale anorexic I expected, Crispo turned out to be a massive, red-haired hooligan with a hefty eggplant where another guy might consider having a nose.

He answered the door in some kind of martial arts outfit, loosely tied so that it exposed an obscenely red nipple poking through the uneven orange carpet on his chest. He opened his mouth and whined something incomprehensible through his lavender proboscis, spraying me with bits of toast. I took this as an invitation to enter.

I followed his orangutan silhouette down a dark hallway into a dusty sitting room crowded with stone-aged furniture.

When my eyes adjusted to the gloom, I realized the room was occupied by a couple of heavily made-up young women who were sitting close together on the couch, smoking.

I wondered how long they had been sitting there. They still had their coats on, but the ashtray on the table before them was pretty full, so I figured that either they had been there a while and were getting ready to leave, or they had just arrived and were already chain-smoking.

Not a good sign.

Refusing the offer of what appeared to be a former chair, I chose instead to sit on the floor near the door in case I needed to leave quickly.

"Pat!" Crispo yelled.

A tiny, lovely young woman with startled brown eyes poked her flower-like head into the room. "Y-y-yes, Crispo, Did you want something, Crispo?"

"My Patsy, Oi loves moi Pat," Crispo brayed lewdly before fixing his Neanderthal gaze on her trembling face.

"Wot's the 'old up with that tea? Fuckit Pat, can't you do anyfing roit? Ah've go' vese loidies 'ere waitin' on the tea, loike." (Okay, that's enough of his appalling accent. You get the picture).

"Y-y-yes, Crispo," said the lovely little head, "It's just that the kettle's got to boil first, or there won't be any tea, hee, hee, because you see it's got to boil first, that's how you make it, I'm sure they understand…oh hello, (she said to me) goodness, how are you?"

I was about to reply, but Crispo cut me off.

"Pat! What're you standing there yapping for? Get the fucking tea!"

We winced collectively as Patsy cracked her head on the doorjamb in her haste to retreat.

One of the girls said, "That's all right, Crispo, I'm sure we can all wait a bit for the tea." Her voice was low and musical. I noticed she wore a lot of expensive looking rings. Her hands were tiny, like paws.

"Oh, yes, I'm all right," lisped her companion.

The one with the jeweled paws turned to me and smiled. "I'm Aura Jane, and this is Carrie."

"I'm just Aura's friend, I'm not doing the gig," explained Carrie, a little hastily, I thought. I found out later that she had been asked, but knew better than to sully her own well-deserved reputation as a singer with a record deal in her future by associating with this trash.

"I'm Evie," I said.

"Oh, you're an American!" Aura Jane exclaimed.

I was surprised that she sounded pleased, after all the months I'd been told disdainfully, "Oh, you're from the *Colonies.*" Like the whole Paul Revere deal was my fault.

Because of her dark coloring and rather posh accent, I thought at first that perhaps Aura Jane was a boarding school bred Italian, but later I found out she came from a well-to-do South African family who probably started out as Arabs. She had liquid black eyes, full lips and a perfect, aquiline nose totally unlike the pug-like features of the typical Englishwoman.

I'd like to note here that I have been warned by phrenologists to stay away from people with big noses. When I think about it, it has certainly proved to be true that all my troubles have been caused by big-nosed people, and Aura Jane was no exception.

Poor little Patsy came back with a loaded tray and fussed over the teapot. Now that her whole body was in the room with us, not just her head, I saw that she was dressed in a shiny black cat suit she had no business wearing. Cat suits are for people who resemble cats. Cat suits are for people who have long, lithe limbs and a predatory attitude.

Patsy was not overweight, but her figure was short and pear-shaped like many English women, and Patsy was anything but predatory.

So it was obvious she was dressing for Crispo, who was likewise dressed inappropriately for what he was. At least he was disgusting, which kind of made the bullshit macho kimono, hey-suck-my-gross-nipple thing work for him.

But Patsy wasn't coming in and snarling, "Here's your fucking tea!"

It was pretty tragic.

While Patsy poured tea and Crispo rummaged around for his tapes and lyrics sheets, Aura Jane quietly took something out of her purse.

"Hey, look at this, Crispo," Aura Jane said.

She wound up and set down a rosy little plastic penis on feet, which hopped across the floor.

Aura Jane watched as Crispo screamed with laughter, her lovely lips twisted in a sly, reptilian smile.

Patsy, whose whole demeanor cried out for a nice flower print dress, a rose garden and a parasol, blushed and gibbered.

I closed my eyes and pretended I was poolside in Ibiza with an airport novel and an umbrella drink.

After the audition (which involved little singing and a lot of having to listen to Crispo talk about how great he was) Aura Jane invited me to her house in Richmond. Since I didn't have any plans except to go drink about sixteen pints of lager at the local pub, I accepted.

I couldn't stop thinking about the expression on her face as she watched Crispo laugh at the little hopping cock.

As she eased her car into traffic, I said, "Was that hopping toy thing a way of pretending to be on Crispo's level, you know, to make him comfortable with us?"

"Don't be daft," she said. "That was my way of telling him, "You are a class-A prick!"

"Brilliant," I said.

We were, like, instant best friends. We stopped to buy a really good bottle of wine, and tooled our merry way out to the suburbs.

The Queenshagger showcase was a hideous flop, which was no surprise to me. Fortunately, the audience consisted mainly of personal friends who teased us for a few weeks, but eventually forgave us for singing really bad songs on stage with an orangutan.

I began spending a lot of time at Aura Jane's house, with my own room and everything. She fed me and washed my clothes and took me to all her really cool gigs. But it soon became apparent that Aura Jane had a strange obsession with me.

Despite the fact that I was not morally superior to anyone we knew, she claimed to perceive in me a purity that seemed to torment her on some level. It had me worried. After all, back then I drank and smoked cigarettes and sometimes hashish like everybody did, and although I tried to be discreet about it, she knew I took lovers from time to time.

Her fixation seemed to do with the fact that I felt I was basically a good person and she felt she was essentially evil. She went on and on about it, how *good* I was and how could I stand to be around someone as *evil* as she. But she'd keep me at her house for sometimes weeks, unable to do without me for some reason I couldn't figure out. I didn't really mind, because in-between her annoying phases of Evie worship, we actually had a pretty great time.

Late one night we had this unnerving conversation.

As usual, we were drinking wine in her kitchen. The table was a mess of tea towels and costume jewelry I had been using to impersonate the Queens of England, and we were drunk and exhausted from laughing.

"How I love you, Evie," Aura Jane began. "You have no idea what you mean to me. I wish I could put you in a little spaceship and keep you in the sky where only I could find you. You'd be my little secret."

I stared at her. "Not this again," I said.

"I just can't figure out how to do it."

"How to do what?" I said, irritated.

"Get you all to myself. You see," she continued, ignoring my discomfort, "if I locked you in your room, you might climb out the window or pick the lock and go home, and I might never see you again. I could put you in the cellar, but you could…dig your way out."

She was tracing a pattern in spilled ashes on the table as she considered her plans to incarcerate me.

"But if I had a little spaceship, you know, a very comfy one…even if you got out, how far could you get? You can't breathe out there in space…yes, a spaceship."

"Aura!" I shouted. "You say you love me, but you want to lock me up? That doesn't sound like love to me."

"You don't understand," she said. "I know you don't." She started to cry.

Oh my god, I thought. *We'll be here until sunrise.*

"I don't have anyone else like you. Who knows when you're going to realize what I'm like and disappear? You're so *good*. How can anyone as *good* as you are be a friend to someone as wicked and evil as me?"

"Aura, stop this. I mean it," I said. "We were having a perfectly nice time until you started this again. I warned you that I would leave if you did this again. I'll get on the night bus right now and go home."

"But you don't have any money," she challenged, smirking.

This was true, since I'd been spending more time with Aunt Jane than working.

"I'm not so good that I wouldn't take some from you by force, if you really piss me off," I said, half jokingly.

That got a small laugh.

"I don't get it," I said. "What is this unforgivable thing you think you've done? I've been around you a lot for a while, and I don't see you doing anything that's so terrible."

"Oh, you don't know, you don't have any idea."

"No, I don't! If you can't tell me, why don't you go to confession? You're a Catholic, aren't you?"

"I can't go to confession," she said. "I can't set foot in a…church. I'm such a sinner! You're not a Catholic, so you can't understand."

She shoved her finger around in the ashes and wept.

"When you are here, I don't feel evil, because you love me. And if you can love a person who will not even be heard by a priest, it must mean you are *good*."

"No," I said angrily. "It means the priest is an ignorant gargoyle preying on the monumental Catholic guilt they planted in your brain when you were a child. Fortunately, I don't have that problem, so why don't you tell me this hideous thing you did and since I'm so fucking *good*, I'll forgive you and we can get back to having fun, all right?" I smacked the arm of my chair for emphasis.

Her eyes grew round and the finger in the ashes tensed in anticipation of the hellfire that would surely arrive to redecorate her kitchen because of my blasphemy.

I started to laugh, imagining her creeping around in the smoldering debris of my body parts trying to figure out how to get breakfast for her family.

"Surely you don't dare speak that way about the church!"

"Yes," I said, "I do dare to criticize the institution responsible for this very annoying conversation."

She took my hand, smearing it with ashes. I let her hold it for a moment.

"You confuse me, Aura," I said gently. "You have so many other friends who are so much more a part of your life and history than I am; how come you don't want to put *them* on comfy little spaceships? I don't get it."

"Because they're not *good* like you," she whispered.

Obviously she wasn't going to let up. I glanced at the clock. It was nearly four in the morning.

"Don't tell me we've run out of wine," I said loudly. "If you're going to keep me up all night abusing my imaginary virtues, you'd better be prepared to give me something to drink."

She laughed through tears and tried to wring a last drop out of the wine bottle. Whenever we ran out of wine but were not done arguing, she would "milk" the bottle and we'd carry on for another hour or so drinking air.

Aura Jane grew increasingly depressed and was capable of going to alarming lengths to get me to go to her. She told me outrageous lies, outrageous in that they were perfectly plausible, knowing her, and I got tired of going down to Richmond every time she told one.

Her husband was drunk and threatening the neighbor children with his carpentry tools! Please come at once!

The arms smuggler she was hiding in the fifth floor bedroom had seduced her and she was afraid she might be pregnant! Please come at once!

It became a pattern.

She'd cry wolf, I'd come running, discover the false alarm, and end up staying with her for weeks.

Inevitably there would come a day when I would suddenly catch her watching me with a gleam in her eye that said, you could have gone home weeks ago, but I've still got you!

In a way I felt it was among my duties to mankind to be there for her, even if it meant putting my own life on hold. In between all the weirdness we had an enormous amount of fun, but I admit that I was often unnerved because she acted as if I was capable of miracles.

A pedestal is a very dangerous place to stand when there are any number of people standing around and only one pedestal. It's not easy to get off a pedestal, if you're stupid enough to get on one in the first place. If you should be callous enough to jump, the zealots below might commit suicide! But if you fall, they will surely trample you into the dust.

Aura Jane sounded terribly upset on the phone, but she wouldn't say why and, as usual, I fell for it. I immediately took the train to Richmond.

"What's going on?" I asked sternly once I'd arrived and was seated in my usual place at her kitchen table, glass of wine in hand.

"What's going on?" she repeated innocently.

"Aura Jane, you were hysterical on the phone. You know perfectly well what I'm talking about."

She had a very peculiar, vaguely familiar expression on her face. It took a minute, but I realized that it reminded me alarmingly of that girl in *The Exorcist*, how her face began to change when the demons were taking over. Hey, I know these things happen in real life. I started to watch Aura Jane more closely.

"Are you all right?" I asked.

"What do you mean, Evie?" she said, normally enough. But her expression continued to change in subtle ways, slowly, like something was moving around under her skin and distorting her features.

Her eyes, which were normally large and liquid bright anyway, seethed with mania.

I knew she didn't take drugs, so I considered mental illness. But could a crazy person be this conniving? I doubted it. I've been around enough crazy people to know that you can always find a flaw in their logic that will ultimately give you control of the situation.

But I wasn't in the mood to play psychological games with Aura Jane in this state. I decided to be confrontational instead. Leaning forward so I could examine her reaction up close, I said, "Hey Aura Jane, you said you had a terrible problem and needed my help."

Aura Jane instantly recoiled into her chair, hands coiled like claws against her chest.

If Gollum had been a young South African beauty with long black hair, this is what he would look like, I thought.

"I never shaid *that,*" she lisped (I might have imagined the lisp). "I don't know what you're *talking* about, snark snark." She gave me a strange, sly smile.

We stared at each other.

She was acting really weird.

Oh my god! She was a Catholic. She thought she was evil. She was always talking about some awful thing she had done, and now she couldn't go to church. Maybe she really was possessed! Well, there was one way to find out. From everything I've read on the subject, if you talk to them directly, demons have to answer you. It's like some kind of supernatural being rule of etiquette, like saying "please" and "thank you" and respecting your elders. I figured if she really was just crazy, she'd think I was being funny and laugh.

"I am speaking to the entity in Aura Jane," I said, fixing her with a stare. "Who are you?"

The reaction was instant and shocking.

She leaped out of her chair so fast it shot away from the table and crashed into the dishwasher.

"Get out!" she screamed. "Get out of this house right this instant!"

"You're possessed, aren't you?" I shouted back. "And you know it!"

"I need you to go away!" she yelled.

"I just spent two hours on the train to get here! I'm not leaving!"

"Oh, yes, you are!" she roared. Then she picked up the wine bottle and hurled it in my direction. It exploded against the cupboards and we were showered with green glass.

The maid came running.

"Oh, oh!" dithered the maid.

"Go back to your room!" Aura Jane screamed at her.

"Oh! Oh!" cried the maid as she pivoted and ran back out of the room.

"YOU!" she shrieked, grabbing a tea towel and beating me with it. "Go, go, go! And don't ever come back!"

Aura Jane flung herself onto her knees in the broken glass. I left her moaning and growling and rolling her eyes on the kitchen floor and went to find the maid.

"Has she been acting this way a lot?" I asked.

"She is not herself, she is a demon," sobbed the maid with a little more dramatic enthusiasm than I felt was required. "A demon," she wept.

The maid! Who, I suddenly realized, was Spanish and also a Catholic!

"Do you really think so?" I asked. "Seriously, do you think she might have a demon?"

She nodded vigorously, grabbing her Rosary and her coat. "It has been a bad week, a very bad week!" She hastened to the door.

"Where are you going?" I asked.

"I go to confession. I tell the priest."

"I'll go with you!"

In the church I had to wait while the maid joined a line of elderly women taking turns in the confessional. I wondered what sins a seventy-year-old woman would have to confess at two-thirty in the afternoon on a Thursday.

"Do you perform exorcisms?" I asked when I managed to corner the priest.

"Oh! Ho, ho, ho. Don't be ridiculous," he said. "They don't teach us all that barbarian superstitious crap anymore."

"Superstitious crap?" I said incredulously. "Isn't it kind of dangerous for someone in your profession to deny the existence of demons?"

"Well, the condition that was believed to be a phenomenon of demonic activity is now considered a treatable mental illness," he said.

"But you've got all these Catholics out there who believe in demons, I mean, the person I want to talk to you about believes she's going to Hell because of them."

"A lot of schizophrenics do believe they are being tormented by the devil. That doesn't mean they are. Has she seen a psychiatrist?"

"Not that I'm aware of," I said. "Look, can't you just talk to her and see what you think?"

"It wouldn't do any good. That's not my area of expertise."

"What exactly *is* your area of expertise?" I knew I was getting a little pushy, but come on, people, know your job description, please!

"I mean, if I go to the doctor and tell him I'm sick, he doesn't just say it's all in my head and send me to a shrink," I said. "He does tests to find out what's wrong with my body."

"That's disgusting," said the priest, walking away. "Perhaps you should consider making a confession yourself."

"What kind of shoemaker would you be if you didn't know how to accurately measure a person's foot?" I went on, determined to make my point.

He walked away faster.

"How can you care for these poor souls you've taught to *fear the devil* if you yourself don't believe in him and you don't know how to tell if a person is possessed?" I basically yelled.

Some hausfraus who had been praying quietly in the pews were now wagging their heads between us, open-mouthed, like we were a tennis match.

"People have been performing exorcisms for thousands of years. Don't you think there might be a reason for it?" I was practically tearing my hair out in frustration.

The priest made it to the exit.

"I'm sorry, I can't help you!" he boomed, and left, slamming the door behind him.

I took the train home and called Westminster Abbey.

"Do you have any exorcists over there?" I asked.

"The Church of England doesn't believe in possession," I was told. "Try the Catholics."

"I did try the Catholics," I said, gritting my teeth. "They don't do exorcisms anymore."

"Well, you might want to call the Vatican."

I toyed with the idea of siccing the Vatican on Aura.

I imagined some forbiddingly robed Cardinal or Bishop striding purposefully up to her door with his whaddyacallit and thingymajigs (I don't know what a Bishop would take on a house call, but I'm sure he'd carry something intimidating to make a lapsed Catholic feel guilt-ridden and condemned).

Then in my mind's eye I saw life fade from her eyes when the bejowled representative of all she feared most in Christendom leaned over her and snarled, "I'm told you're possessed by a demon, ingrate! Are you trying to ruin the reputation of the Catholic Church?"

Okay, too over the top.

Instead I imagined a slim, black-robed priest with haunted eyes, saying, "I will take the demon in myself, just to help you, poor child."

Nope. She'd just give him a cup of tea, flirt with him for a few minutes, and send him on his way.

Oh, come on, Evie, I told myself. I've had rather a lot of experience with the occult, traveling in strange places as I have, but really, for all I knew, her psycho behavior could be due to imminent organ shutdown brought on by too many port-and-brandies. How could I help her?

Considering the difficulty I was having with the experts, I figured shooting her in the head like a rabid dog would be a lot easier, and went to buy a gun.

Just kidding.

I decided to ignore Aura Jane for a while. Then I decided I couldn't leave her alone in that state. I called her house a few times. She wouldn't answer the phone. I tried calling a few more churches.

One priest said, "Look, I'm only a priest because I'm the youngest son and that's our tradition. I don't have any experience with what you're talking about."

Yeah, that's what he said! I'm telling you, we're in trouble folks.

I couldn't stop thinking about Aura Jane. I had terrible nightmares about groaning abysses. I burst into tears for no reason. I started going to church, something I had not done in years.

One day I got a phone call from Mickey, a recording engineer I worked with sometimes. He was an old alcoholic with questionable hearing, but I loved him because he gave me a lot of work and he knew The Beatles and once got me some recording time at Abbey Road Studios.

"I heard you were looking for an exorcist," said Mick.

"I was, but I've given up. There aren't any," I said.

"Why, yes, there are," he said. "There is one."

"How do you know?"

"He's a friend of mine."

"No! Really?"

"He doesn't practice anymore, because nobody believes in the devil these days, but he still has a vicarage in London."

I couldn't very well ask Mick to introduce me to the exorcist without telling him what the problem was, so I explained the situation as discreetly as possible, hoping he wouldn't laugh at me. He didn't, bless him. He listened with seriousness and respect, and told me where I could find the exorcist.

"I must say Aura Jane is quite lucky to have a friend like you. From what I understand, possession is a terrible experience. It could be she has some other problem as you say, but it seems to me the exorcist is the only person who would know for certain. I will let him know you are coming by."

"Thank you," I said.

Well, if nothing else, I thought, *this will certainly be interesting.*

I went to the ancient, freaky church where the exorcist lived. I was nervous. It seemed like the moment I stepped from the sidewalk onto the property, the whole world got darker. There aren't any wolves in London, but I still half expected to hear one howl. That's how Alfred Hitchcock this place was.

The stone walls were so old they wept and it wasn't even raining for once. Gnarled tree roots had buckled the ground into a strange landscape dotted with wild grasses. The vines were completely out of control. I crept up the front path and hoped they weren't carnivorous.

The only depiction of an exorcist I'd ever seen was the actor in the movie, so I kind of expected (or I was hoping, to be honest) the exorcist to be a swarthy, handsome man whose spiritual torment only I could relieve with my great compassion, gentle wit, and Frederick's of Hollywood underwear.

That fun little fantasy soon bit the dust!

The exorcist wore the robes of a priest, but he reminded me of the mole-rat dude in that movie *Atlantis*, with a little Ed Asner thrown in, if you know what I mean. He was short, rotund, and about seventy, and he wouldn't look me in the eye. I assumed this was because he didn't want to gamma-ray me to death with his "boss of the demons" powers.

"I think my friend is possessed," I blurted out.

"Come in and tell me why you think so," whispered the old exorcist.

He led me into what I thought was a tiny room lined with books, until I realized it was an enormous room so packed with books there was only a tiny space left to sit in. I sat opposite the exorcist with our knees almost touching in this tower of books.

He saw me looking around.

"These are the records of this church," he said. "They go back nearly two thousand years. This church was built soon after the crucifixion."

"That explains the state of the garden," I joked.

"What?"

"Nothing. Has there always been an exorcist here?" I asked.

"Yes, and each one taught by the one before. Our line goes back to Christ, himself. I was chosen, and have performed that service as one of my duties here in this vicarage for many years."

I couldn't help but goggle over that. This exorcist was obviously the real deal, with training that came down from guys who learned it from Christ, himself. How lucky could I get?

Now I was really bummed that he wasn't a hot babe.

We sat down amongst the books, and he poured us both a generous glass of Communion wine.

I told him about Aura Jane, her Catholic self-loathing, the changes I'd seen in her over the past months and our bizarre final confrontation. I told him about my nightmares.

"I figured an exorcist might be able to tell me what was what," I said.

"I would need to see her to know for sure," he said, watching me solemnly.

"She won't come," I explained. "She's terrified of priests. I told you, I couldn't get her to go to church or confession or anything."

"Well, if she is possessed, that would be normal. But then, a lot of people don't want to go to church anymore."

"So what can we do?" I asked.

"Demons are very mischievous, but they are stupid and notoriously bad liars. We will have to trick them. But first I will perform an exorcism on you."

"What?"

"Yes. Whatever is tormenting her has spread its dark tentacles out to you. You may not be possessed, but you are obsessed, you are having bad dreams, you look haunted. Besides, I haven't had an opportunity to perform my duties in a long time."

"But *you* said I'm not possessed!" I said, nervously gulping the last of my communion wine.

"Of course not. But I see the darkness, which surrounds you and this I can dispel. If there is demonic influence at work here, we will get to the bottom of it shortly. Do you agree?"

"Well, okay, but can I have a little more wine first?"

The exorcist led me down some worn, ancient stairs into the crypt, deep under the ancient building, where there was total darkness.

He lit some candles and left me there to freak out quietly by myself for a long few minutes. I could hear the wind howling and whispering through the stones. It was muggy and damp, and I could smell water.

The exorcist came back wearing an elaborately embroidered robe and some kind of special exorcist hat. He arranged some things on the altar, a couple of books, a vial of something that could only be holy water, and a bunch of crucifixes.

Then he made me kneel in front of him, placed his hands on my head, and, after drawing a loud, deep breath, started shouting angrily in Latin.

That's the last thing I remember.

* * *

When I came to, I was sitting on the cold stone floor. My face felt bruised, and my hair was a total mess. Dang! It would take hours to comb out.

The exorcist, back in his priest outfit, was sitting patiently beside me.

"What happened?" I whispered.

"We were successful. The dark forces have departed. How do you feel?"

"Was I possessed?" I said.

"No, but I do believe your friend, Aura Jane, may be. You are a very sensitive young lady with a good heart, attractive to demonic entities. That's why Aura Jane would want you close to her, as you have described."

"I feel really weird right now," I told him.

"That is normal," said the old exorcist. "You will need to go home and rest for a few days. Drink a lot of water."

"Okay," I said.

"We need to figure out how I can see this friend of yours."

"I could take you to one of her gigs, but she's not answering her phone right now so I don't know if she's singing anywhere."

"I have an idea," said the old exorcist.

"What is it?"

"Have you ever been baptized?"

"I'm not sure. I doubt it," I said. "My parents had bad experiences with religion."

"Well, this is how I can help you in two ways. It is helpful to follow an exorcism with a baptism. You should be baptized anyway. Also, it is very rude not to attend a ritual of the church, baptism, wedding, funeral, whatnot, when one is invited to do so. We will arrange your baptism. You will invite your friend, Aura Jane. If she comes, perhaps I can have a word with her. If she doesn't, you at least will be all right."

I called Aura Jane's house. At last she answered.

"It's me," I said.

She didn't say anything.
"You'll be receiving an invitation in the mail," I said.
"Are you getting married?" she asked.
"No, I'm getting baptized."
She immediately put the phone down.

Aura Jane did not show up, and I never saw her again.

But that is how I was saved from the demons, and came to be baptized in one of London's oldest churches. The rare sun came out that day as I bowed over an ancient stone font. Holy water was scooped onto my head with a beautiful abalone shell, held in the hand of the last living exorcist in England, last in a long line that came down from Christ himself.

I'd love to say that ever since then I've been nothing short of a living saint, but hey, how much fun is that?

CULTURE SHOCK

The urge to survive is extremely powerful, but it's pretty obvious to me that the urge to survive is rarely accompanied by anything remotely like common sense. We would not have expressions like "out of the frying pan, into the fire", unless enough of our pre-supermarket ancestors had seen something they were planning to eat make exactly that bold but fatal move. Well, now we may not see our packaged chicken pecking and clawing its way out of the microwave, but we so-called human beings have obviously not evolved past indulging in this idiotic behavior ourselves when life becomes too uncomfortable.

And so it was with me.

After the business with Aura Jane and the exorcist, I spent a few weeks in hiding. I didn't want to be in England anymore. I needed to come up with a plan.

I hid in the warmth of my bed, peering out into the freezing English gloom from the cave of blankets like a hermit crab in its borrowed shell.

When I could no longer stand my own smell I moved my operation to the bathtub, where I lurked in expensive clouds of steam (remember the coin operated meters from the last story) until the pickled state of my skin inspired me to go to the local pub, where I sat in dark corners nibbling shrimp flavored crisps and sipping warm lager.

I went from bed to bath to pub and back to bed. When I got bored with that routine I took to skulking under my piano with a crossword puzzle.

I guess I was waiting for something to happen.

I must have been, because when it happened, I reacted as if I had been waiting for it to happen.

I don't know why, but one day when I was under the piano studying a particularly fascinating dust bunny, I was struck by an interesting idea. Hey, why not go back to America?

I sat up so suddenly I whacked my head on the piano and the strings inside it made a quiet, dissonant *bong* that vibrated in my brain. Talk about for whom the bell tolls! Just then the front door's mail slot rattled and I heard the irrational envelope of possible salvation land heavily on the parquet. It was a letter from a friend in Los Angeles. I crawled back under the piano to read it.

Roberto, a sound engineer I knew, was inviting me to Los Angeles, which he described as an idyllic place of glistening palm trees and pristine beaches. He wrote of the famous musicians he worked with, the movie stars he brushed elbows with, the scent of hot jasmine rising from Dr. Seussian topiary and days of sunlight without end. Come, thou talented if slightly fucked up genius! Come and get famous in Los Angeles! Yes!

This was obviously fate at work.

But wait.

Every time I acted on a tip from fate, the result was more like the punch line of a cruel joke.

But that could be my fault. Maybe I was misinterpreting the signs. Maybe what I thought was serendipitous guidance from above was actually cleverly disguised bait from the *other guy*. Why else would I have become the girl who was baptized by the last exorcist in England and was now playing with dust under her piano?

But maybe I was making too much of this. After all, why would the devil, who hadn't been having much luck with me so far, continue to focus his diabolical attention on a mere wannabe do-gooder like me?

I decided I was paranoid and ungrateful.

Clearly the angels were trying to help me out.

Besides, I had never been to California, where people have nothing to do but go surfing by day and congratulate each other at awards parties every night. I might even get a tan.

Okay, I would be putting myself among strangers in a new city. But hadn't I already successfully navigated my way around the world? Wasn't I accustomed to the curious discomfort of being a foreigner? *If I can survive this, surely I can survive that*, I thought. Plus it was getting boring under the piano.

I had an aunt in California. I was reasonably sure she'd put me up for a while if necessary.

Roberto the sound engineer said he'd introduce me to the right people. He was absolutely sure he could get me a record deal in America. It seemed I had nothing to lose.

And so, using the faulty logic of the doomed crustacean, I crawled to the edge of the proverbial frying pan and bought a first class plane ticket into the fire.

The first indication that I was in unfamiliar territory had to do with the American attitude towards alcohol, which in Europe is a much discussed and celebrated part of the culture.

In Europe, a five-year-old can be sent out to buy a bottle of wine for the family's lunch or dinner. If the five-year-old happens to drink the wine instead of taking it home to share with his parents, everybody just laughs and gets on with their day.

"Oh, ho, ho, did you hear? Little Giuseppe guzzled the new Bella and had to be sent back for a new bottle! I guess lunch will be an hour late today!"

In America, if a kid asks for a sip of Mommy's holiday eggnog or champagne, he is taken straight to the nearest child psychologist, because obviously something is terribly wrong.

"Do you know why you're here, kid?" asks the overpaid, myopically sun-deprived psychologist.

"Um, I wanted to taste the wine?" says the clueless kid.

"Yes, and now we're going to figure out why you would want to do such a thing. This here is an anatomically correct dolly for you to play with. Has anyone ever touched your privates, son?"

"Well, my mother used to change my diaper and now she gives me a bath every night before she tucks me in and reads me a story."

Aha! thinks the shrink. *The child has been molested. No wonder he is an alcoholic!*

Twenty years later, the kid is addled by the combination of psychoanalysis and prescription drugs, and his good judgment has been lost. He has molested twelve anatomically correct children, but now he is old enough to blame for his own actions. Mommy, whose last precious memory of blissful family life has been sullied by my exaggerated, sordid diversion from the story, is off the hook.

She may be on her way to suicide because the stuff *she* is taking for depression makes her unable to forget that she is to blame for birthing a criminal into the carefully ordered world of society. At least Mommy can lapse into the comforting self pity of shopping for badly made shoes between turns to cry on television.

My God! So many lives tragically ruined, so many closets filled with trash because an innocent little child wanted to taste the wine!

Okay, okay.

So, when I got off the plane in Los Angeles after the long transatlantic flight from London, I was exhausted and I wanted a glass of beer. Even more so when I stepped out of the airport and was slammed in the face by the muggy breeze, smelling of the ocean, flowers, and the underlying, pervasive nastiness common to all big cities.

After living in rainy, cold London for so long I was totally ecstatic to see palm trees gleaming in strong, blinding sunlight. But it was hot! Now I *really* wanted a beer.

Now, for those of you who were born yesterday, ever since those Belgian monks accidentally let their stash of barley rot in the cellar while they were trying to control the soulless homunculus they had created using what was clearly a sketchy understanding of alchemy, beer has been a big deal in most parts of the Christian world. Beer, when it is made properly, is considered a food, a drink, and is given to pregnant women in Ireland as a tonic to fortify the blood and make labor easier.

Beer is our friend!

"Please, Auntie Jet, can we stop someplace and have a beer?" I asked my aunt, who had come to fetch me from the airport.

(I didn't know her very well. I was in for some surprises).

"Oh, honey," my aunt sighed. "I know my sister didn't raise you right and you've been living amongst the heathen overseas, but Jesus doesn't want you to drink alcohol. I've already had six of our family members committed to the psychiatric ward because of alcoholism. How about a nice double bacon burger with extra cheese instead? I bet it's been a long while since you saw any *real* food."

This is when I realized I was in deep trouble.

Forget about a relaxing and medicinally nutritious drink—had I eaten my last legume? Had I, by coming back to the United States, accidentally doomed myself to a life of weirdness and nonsense? Were my days of innocent healthful enjoyment over? Had I, by stepping back onto American soil, accidentally abandoned my rights and given Aunt Jet the power to commit me to a psychiatric ward because I wanted a beer?

I decided not to think about that right now.

"Auntie Jet, I've just flown halfway around the world. I'm tired. I really just want a beer and a bed."

"Well, I feel real bad for you, but I just don't want to be an enabler! Here, why don't you take one of my pills instead? Let's see. I've got painkillers from my accident and mood regulators for my depression and muscle relaxers for my tension and some estrogen because my hormones are out of whack." She popped a few pills herself and washed them down with a can of diet soda.

"Are you okay to drive?" I asked when her eyes glazed over and I realized we were going about 30 miles per hour *under* the posted speed limit.

"Of course I'm okay! It's just that you have to be really careful driving around here, because of all the drug addicts."

Oh my god!

Putting on my best snooty British accent, I proceeded to harangue my aunt with how I was a grown woman who could do as I pleased and as far as I knew, Jesus, who went around turning perfectly good water into wine and offering it as a blood substitute to the vampires posing as his disciples, was just as much a lush as the rest of us. Finally, she gave in just to shut me up.

We stopped at a convenience store where the only brewed beverages available were thin, scorched American coffee that smelled like stewed burlap and its evil twin, a fermented rice concoction they called "The King of American Beers."

Well, when in Rome, as they say.

I tried to buy a can of Budweiser.

When I put the can on the counter, the Filipino clerk narrowed his eyes suspiciously and reached under the counter for his gun.

"Do you have some identification?"

"What do you want to see identification for? I'm just buying a beer."

"You have to be twenty-one to buy beer. Everybody knows that."

"Look at me. Can't you see I'm over twenty-one?"

"Lots of people get plastic surgery," said the clerk. "I need to see your California driver's license."

"I don't have a California driver's license! I'm from England!"

"If you don't have a valid driver's license, I can't sell you this beer."

"That's ridiculous. Here's my passport," I said, handing it to him.

"I thought you said you were from England."

"I'm American. I live in England."

"You don't sound American."

"Neither do you!"

He spent about ten minutes reading the small print and checking out the weird looking stamps that proved I had been allowed by international government into all sorts of dens of iniquity.

"This is no good," he finally said.

"Why not?" I yelled. "It's a federally issued document of identification! I can get into any country in the world with that thing, but you won't sell me a can of beer?"

He picked up the phone and dialed 911.

"Send the cops! I've got a foreign terrorist in my store trying to buy beer!"

"Okay, okay! Forget it."

I went back to the car.

"Everything all right?" asked my aunt. "Where's your beer?"

"I changed my mind."

"Praise the Lord! But honey, you don't look so good. Are you sure you don't want a pill?"

"That's okay, thanks. I think I'm just having culture shock," I said.

"Well, you might need to drink some water. I keep seven gallons of water in the trunk in case of emergency. That's why the car is so heavy."

"What kind of emergency requires seven gallons of water?" I asked my aunt.

I could have been imagining things, but I thought I saw her eyeballs jiggle disturbingly for a second.

"You never know what's going to happen in California," she whispered, looking like she was about to cry. "We have earthquakes. And if you get stranded out in the desert where I live, you can die in twenty minutes from dehydration."

"Where am I, Saudi Arabia? I thought I was in California! The land of vineyards and Malibu Barbie! What do you mean you can die of dehydration in twenty minutes?"

"It's different in the desert," she said ominously. "You'll see."

Aunt Jet slowed the car even more to protect her precious cargo of water. The cars behind us changed lanes and sped past with a lot of honking and swearing.

"That's another thing you have to be careful about," Aunt Jet warbled over the din, "road rage. People shoot each other on the freeway all the time."

I hunched down in my seat and waited for the hail of bullets we were certain to be attracting at this pace.

My aunt lived way out in the desert east of Los Angeles. We had decided I would stay with her and her new husband until I got acclimated and felt ready to take on Hollywood. But I was already pretty sure I would never adjust, and it was only my first day.

I should have stayed in Thailand! I should have moved back to Paris! I should have let Aura put me in a spaceship! Why, oh why, did I come back to America?

When we stopped to pee I snuck to a pay phone and called my friend Roberto in Hollywood.

"I think I'm going to have to go home to England," I said.

"No! Come on, Evie, give it a chance!" said Roberto.

"I did already and I don't like it here, it's too weird. I feel like I've died and gone to hell. People take pills for everything, but think you're an alcoholic if you want beer in the middle of the afternoon! People eat plastic cheese and shoot at each other from their cars! You can die of dehydration in twenty minutes!"

Roberto laughed. "You're not going to die of dehydration! Just hang there and enjoy your aunt for a couple of days. The desert's great. I'll come down and get you this weekend. And you'll like Los Angeles, you really will."

"Are you sure?"

"Yes. You just need to get around the musicians, be with your own kind. Your music will do really well here, because it's so *original* and *sophisticated.*"

"Are you sure?" I said again.

"Look, just give it six months," he said. "I believe I can get you a record deal. I've already set up some meetings. Spend a few days with your aunt and I will come and get you."

I thought about it. *I may be in hell,* I decided. *But at least it's nice and warm here.*

"Okay," I finally said.

I had never met my aunt's eighth husband. He called himself "Hellcat", but his real name was Egbert. I didn't know it at the time, but he was a tweaker. For those of you with your heads in the sand, a tweaker is someone who uses a dangerous, super-addictive drug made out of cough syrup. It leaches all the calcium out of your bones and dissolves your teeth. I had never been around any addicts before, so I didn't recognize the signs. I just thought he was a nervous hillbilly whose dentist needed to rethink his career choice.

Jet and Hellcat's ramshackle little house squatted in the middle of a glaring landscape of sand devils and dead wind-battered bushes. We seemed to be in a vast dust bowl surrounded by low mountains that looked exactly like the top of a meringue pie.

"Wow, Aunt Jet, this is just like being on Mars."

"I know," she said darkly, and popped another painkiller.

We parked under the only living vegetation I could see, an enormous grapefruit tree near the house that was dropping giant yellow globes all over a collection of rusty cars with shattered windshields and missing wheels.

"Is Hellcat a mechanic?" I asked.

"No, he's a carpenter. Those are our old cars. We sure do go through cars! The desert just eats them right up. Hellcat hasn't had time to get them fixed since he got out of rehab because we've been so busy working on the house."

"Rehab? Was he in an accident?"

"Why do you ask if he was in an accident? I said he was in rehab." She stared at me and I realized that although we were both speaking English, we were not communicating.

Okay!

I noticed a long shiny thing sticking out of the sand that looked a lot like the top of a bus.

"What's that?" I asked Aunt Jet.

"It's the top of a bus," said Jet. "Hellcat buried it out here last month."

"Did he let the people out first?" I asked.

"What?"

"Nothing."

"Swamp coolers just don't work that well out here in the desert (*maybe that's why they're called swamp coolers,* I thought), so he thought we could turn the bus into an underground room where we could get out of the heat. He dug a tunnel between the house and the bus so we wouldn't have to walk outside during the worst of it."

"Did it work?"

"No, it's hotter than blazes down there. Now we use it as an oven so we don't have to cook in the house. I have a chicken roasting in there now."

In Thailand I had eaten chicken cooked inside a coconut and a coffee can, and I thought that was a fun thing to tell people. Now I had an even better one. I've eaten chicken that was cooked in a bus buried in the California desert! Bet you can't top that.

"Why don't you grab your luggage and bring it around back. I'll go in first and you can hand it to me and then you can come in."

This didn't make any sense.

"Um, why can't I just take it in the door?"

"Oh. We have to go around back and climb in the window because Hellcat nailed all the doors shut."

"Why did he do that?" I asked.

"Because of all the drug addicts around here."

"Not more drug addicts," I said.

"Oh, yes. Drugs are a big problem in the desert."

"So," I said, "how about I unpack my things and take a walk? It looks like it would be kind of fun to explore around here."

"I wouldn't do that if I were you, unless you have some good boots and a stick."

"Why not? I don't see any drug addicts."

She almost laughed. Almost.

"Scorpions. They're all over the place. Mountain lions. And you have to be real careful of the snakes. Just the other day a rattler got into the house and I had to kill it with a shovel."

"How did the snake get into the house if all the doors are nailed shut?" I said.

"I think it came up the tunnel from the bus."

"How did the snake get in the bus?"

"I don't know," she sighed, obviously tired of my questions.

We went round the back and I helped my hefty aunt clamber through the window. Then I passed my luggage through to her and climbed in myself. Then I had to just stand there for a while. It was black as pitch in the house.

"Where are you?" I asked nervously.

"I'm right here," said my aunt, making me jump. She was standing right next to me.

"Why is it so dark in here? Don't you have any electricity?"

"Yes, but if it's dark it seems cooler. You wouldn't believe how expensive those swamp coolers are to run twenty-four hours a day. I don't know why I'm so fat 'cause we can't hardly afford to eat because of them swamp coolers. Thank god for the dollar menu at McDonald's! Just wait a minute. Your eyes will adjust."

We stood in the darkness. I opened my eyes as wide as possible, then closed them. It didn't make any difference. It was still dark. Then I became aware of a strange noise, like a distant whooshing filled with a tiny patter of clicks.

"What's that sound?" I whispered.

"That's the other reason, besides the heat, I never use the kitchen. That's cockroaches."

I stared in the general direction of her face, horrified.

"Can't you call an exterminator or something?" I said.

"We did. The exterminator said he thinks they're a mutation. They're immune to everything he tried. They do nuclear testing out here, you know."

"What about violence, are they immune to that?"

"No, they sure aren't," she laughed. "Hellcat wore out three pairs of work boots trying to crush them to death but they breed faster than we can kill them. So we gave up. We can't afford to keep buying him new boots."

"Have you ever considered moving to someplace a little less scary, a little cooler, maybe closer to civilization?"

"Yeah, I think about it all the time," she said. "I just don't have the energy."

The next morning Aunt Jet went to church so I got to hang out with Uncle Hellcat.

We sat in the dark living room listening to the mutant cockroaches whirring and clicking on the other side of the house.

"Ahem!" said Hellcat in a friendly way.

I coughed a little back.

"Jet told me you like beer," he finally said.

"Yes," I said.

"Well, she don't like me drinking or nothing but I got a secret stash and I'll share it with you if you promise not to tell on me."

"Okay," I said. He climbed out of the window with a shovel and dug up a couple of beers.

"They might be a little warm, cause I didn't bury em deep like I should. She hardly ever leaves the house and she never stays gone long so I got to be able to move it quick."

We brushed the sand off and drank the warm beer.

"So, where are you from, Uncle Hellcat? I don't recognize your accent."

"*I* got an accent?" He laughed, and I saw his three teeth gleaming in the darkness. "You're the one with the accent! Har, har har har har!"

"Ha ha ha!" I said. "So, uh, where are you from, Hellcat?"

"Back east. I'm from the Ozarks."

"Oh. Isn't that where the Bigfoot live?"

I was only joking, but he said, "Yeah, but they're not the problem. They're actually real gentle. No, the real problem up there is the aliens. They're always messing with folks up there. The government knows but they won't do nothing. You ever see a flying saucer?"

"No, but my sister was abducted by aliens once." I said helpfully, glad to have found some common ground.

"Me, too!" said Uncle Hellcat. "Did they put one of them doohickeys in her eye?"

"I don't think so," I said. "But she had a baby and they took it."

"Oh, she's part of the breeding program," he said, nodding sagely. He was clearly an expert on alien activities.

We drank the warm beer.

"Why did you move out here to the desert?" I asked.

"I didn't. Well, not on purpose, har har." He slurped some more beer. "I was trying to get to Mexico 'cause I killed a guy, but then I met your aunt and she said she'd let me move in with her if I got off the drugs, so I went to rehab and we got married."

I was glad it was dark so he couldn't see the expression on my face.

"Who did you kill?" I said, as casually as possible.

"A guy I was doing drugs with up in the mountains. We were really fucked up and we got in a argument and he pissed me off so I smashed his head in with a rock. Then I figured, uh-oh, time to get out of here for a while! Har har har!"

"Oh my god!"

"Oh, don't worry, it turned out okay. Nobody ever came after me. Don't guess he was ever even found. I buried him up there."

"Oh," I said. "Good idea."

"Lotsa bodies in the desert, too, you know."

"Really?"

"Oh, sure, this is where all the murderers dump their victims. You go out into the desert, man, there's skeletons all over the place. Some smart guy could make a fortune selling 'em to the schools for that anatomy class." Uncle Hellcat finished his beer and rolled the empty bottle into the black abyss under the couch.

"He'd have a hard time explaining where he was getting all those skeletons," I said.

"Yeah, somebody might think to ID the teeth or something and find out it was one a them missing persons on the milk cartons."

"People might think he killed 'em all himself," I said.

"Yeah! Har har har!"

"Har har har!" I said.

"We got a little more time before your aunt comes back from church. You want another brewsky?"

"Sure," I said. "Why not?"

Uncle Hellcat picked up the shovel and went back out into the yard to dig up another couple of brewskies.

PARTY LIKE A ROCK STAR

My first Christmas in Los Angeles, Roberto the sound engineer and I were invited to the annual Christmas party at the recording studios in Hollywood where we were doing most of our work.

"This is going to be great, Evie. You're going to meet all the right people at this party. There's this producer I want you to meet. His name is Shrimp. Best ears in the business. He's going to be there, so bring the best of the stuff you recorded in England."

Totally excited, I promptly went out to shop for something fabulous on Melrose, which is where all the L.A. rockers bought their clothes until they could afford their own designer.

On the night of the party we got all dressed up, picked up some friends who were coming with us, and drove over to the studio.

You could hear the music a mile away, and the loud, stupid laughter of the stoned ricocheting off the jacaranda and eucalyptus trees.

We drove up to the gate and were buzzed in.

The floating wreaths of skunk-smelling smoke were so thick we got a contact high as soon as we stepped out of the car, which was taken away and parked by a giggling Mexican valet in a red vest, who I would have sworn was on acid.

Roberto, sweating from performance anxiety, wiped his face on his sleeve, staining the maroon silk.

"Ready, Evie?" he said to me. "You look great."

It wasn't even ten o'clock, and already shrieking young women were starting to throw their clothes atop the landscaping while rock stars took turns ducking into the producers' lounges for a quick blow job. The hit making producers themselves were visible through the soundproofed glass of one of the control rooms, head banging to next year's Billboard Top Ten and talking shop.

Since I was still suffering from the effects of the acute snobbism I'd been subjected to during my years in England I found the scene a little overwhelming, but it was exciting to be part of what was left of the crazy rock and roll free-for-all I'd missed out on in the previous decade, which I had spent masquerading first as a schoolgirl and then as a European aristocrat.

It wouldn't be long before there was a crackdown in Hollywood on this sort of behavior, with everyone going into Twelve Step programs and getting all serious about "business," but back then if you were in on the L.A. rock scene you were expected to be irresponsible and shocking and throw up on people every chance you got. And if for some reason you didn't or couldn't drink or do the drug in fashion you'd better have some weird sexual perversion, because otherwise everybody would know you were a fraud and laugh your ass right out of town.

I am convinced that the reason there are now more psychologists than lawyers in L.A. is because things just aren't fun anymore. It seems like people are just going through the motions. Up until things changed in the '90s, when it became possible to record yourself at home and the record labels started to die off because they were scared into signing only "Song writing for Dummies" type formula drivel written by fired A&R executives, it was still very exciting to be a recording artist in Los Angeles. Everybody wanted to either be one or be around one.

Nowadays, if you're a musician lucky enough to get a meeting, you show up in a suit with a business plan and a website, and god help you if you've ever had a DUI. But back then *amp rentals* on your invoice meant hookers were paid for by the studio, and there was still a lot of wild behavior, tight pants and snorting and gibbering and screwing anything that twitched. You could be the biggest idiot in the world and still get the big bucks if you could scream on pitch and were willing to drink something that had been stirred with someone else's dick. We loved it.

We milled around the patio with drinks, picking at the mountains of food on every surface and dropped into the conversations of glassy-eyed, grinning people more famous than us.

The bass player of a superstar rock band, whom I had met on a couple of occasions, staggered over to me.

"Hey!" he crowed, leering at me through his tangle of hair.

"How's the new record going?" I asked.

He burst into sputtering giggles and splashed his cocktail around, rings and studs winking in the colored spotlights of the garden.

"Hrrblp mmmhnn ha ha ha gablurpy blah!" he shouted, banging me on the shoulder with glee. He obviously thought he was making sense, so I played along.

"That's great, great!" I said.

"PPlbp gshwertny furshibble, ha ha, shit!" he said.

His skinny, platinum blonde wifelet tottered over on six-inch heels, swathed in feather boas.

"I love you, honey!" she squealed, and promptly crashed down on the tiles in a tangle of ostrich plumes. The bass player leaned over unsteadily to try to help her up, and fell on top of her. They promptly forgot about me and lay there in a heap smooching and licking their spilled drinks off each other.

I went to find Roberto, who was talking to an enormous bespectacled man, who turned out to be Shrimp, and his tiny muscular wife, Cupcake, who was white-knuckling a wine glass and staring around the party with her perfect teeth clenched in a forced grin. Roberto saw me and grabbed my arm.

"This is the girl I've been telling you about, Shrimp. She's amazing, just amazing. Child prodigy, classically trained, killer rock songs. Superstar material, totally unique."

"Uh, thanks," I said uncomfortably.

Roberto reversed the direction of his sales pitch, practically dancing with nerves.

"This is the guy I was telling you about, Evie. Shrimp is a great producer! Works with everybody, Barbra, Mariah, Whitney, you name it. Best ears in the business."

"Thanks, thanks, man," wheezed the Shrimp.

"Hi!" I said, and shook the Shrimp's damp, pie dough hand.

"Best ears in the business," Roberto said again, licking sweat off his upper lip.

"Evie, this is Shrimp's wife, Cupcake. I've been dying to introduce you two, Cupcake. You and Evie have a lot in common. I know you'll get along just great!"

"You don't say," said Cupcake, and stared at my hand for a second as if it was some festering nasty thing she'd found clogging her toilet.

Cupcake's handshake was like a vise, which surprised me because from the way her eyes wandered I'd assumed she wasn't all there. When she let go my hand felt like it had been slammed in a car door. I surreptitiously checked for broken bones.

"There are some interesting skull shapes here tonight," Cupcake commented, gazing around at the revelers with a slight sneer. "Let's see, there's an Australopithecus over there, yep and another one."

"Ha, ha! She's so funny," cackled Shrimp, gazing fondly at his wife. "Australopithecus! Ha!"

I caught sight of the young men in question, who were unbelievably cute longhairs sharing a bong under a banana tree.

"They look like Homo Erectus to me," I said weakly.

"You mean 'sapiens', right?" said the Shrimp.

"Those are the guys from 'The Rump Roasters,' that hot new band out of Texas," Roberto informed us. He sounded pleasant enough, but his eyes zigzagged back and forth between me and the heavenly young stoners with totally justified suspicion.

"The Rump Roasters?" I murmured, drooling.

Roberto glared at me.

"Neanderthal at seven o'clock," announced Cupcake.

Suddenly her glass shattered from the pressure of her fingers, spraying us with wine and shards of glass.

"Darn, that's the third time," she mumbled through her teeth, completely unfazed.

"Ha, ha, ha! She's so cool!" bellowed the Shrimp.

"Ha, ha, ha! Hilarious!" crowed Roberto.

"Ha, ha, ha" I said, eyeing Cupcake nervously. I stepped back a few inches.

"I'll get you another one, Cupcake," said Roberto, and loped off to the bar.

"Thanks, Roberto," said Cupcake, feigning politeness as she wiped a few drops of Roberto's sweat out of her eye with a cocktail napkin.

"So Roberto said you have a tape for me," said Shrimp, bobbing congenially. "I'll listen to it later and what I'll do is, uh, I'll call ya."

"Oh, thank you," I said. "That'd be great."

"Oh yeah, man," said Roberto, handing Cupcake another glass of wine. "This is great man, you're going to love her!"

I set my drink on a table and dug in my bag for the tape, which I forked over to Shrimp while Roberto rhapsodized some more about how wonderful I was, how talented, how beautiful, how unique my music.

"Very excited, very excited," said Shrimp, doing his best to look excited. He pocketed the tape containing the precious fruit of my years of suffering and hard labor.

"Yes, wonderful," said Cupcake, a little sarcastically I thought. "I just can't *wait* to have you guys up to the house."

Finally, after one of the expensive mixing boards had been damaged by the shenanigans of an overenthusiastic leather-clad couple and the missing hookers had been located playing shower games in the studio's large bathroom with a married producer, the studio's owner announced the end of the party and kicked everybody out.

"We'll have a cleaning crew in here for a month before we can open again," he gloated, waving his cigar gleefully in my face. "This is the best party we've ever had!"

"Great party, great party!" everyone who could still speak agreed.

We followed the tottering crowd out to the parking lot amidst cries of, "Call me tomorrow! Don't forget!" and, "It's a deal, be at my office tomorrow!" and, "I love you, Honey!"

Roberto and I, giddy from the copious amounts of champagne with which we'd toasted our impending success, found our friends in the parking lot, talking to the cute Texans from The Rump Roasters.

"What's everybody doing now?" said our friends. "We're not ready to go home yet."

Neither was I! I needed time to figure out how to get one (or all!) of those luscious babes to meet me in a hotel room as soon as possible without Roberto finding out.

We agreed to meet over at a local Industry hangout, a tiny dark bar called the Snake Pit over on Melrose, and caravanned woozily down the street in our cars, which were miraculously unscathed by the acidhead valet in the red vest.

The Snake Pit was usually crammed and spilling various types of entertainment weirdos onto the sidewalk, but it was pretty late so we were able to get a table.

Roberto, me, our friends, and The Rump Roasters crammed around a smelly table and screamed drinks orders at a snotty actress wearing a dress the size of a handkerchief, who zipped around dangerously balancing full drink trays on three fingers over our heads while stuffing tips in her cleavage.

The bar was so loud and everyone was so stoned we couldn't talk to each other. I didn't care. I was perfectly happy to sit there and ogle the eye candy across the table from me, the four members of "The Rump Roasters."

The most beautiful of them, who, thanks to some sly detective work back at the party, I now knew was the lead guitarist, looked up just then and we locked eyes.

His mouth fell open as he was apparently stunned by the unexpected sight of my exquisite beauty. I was instantly lobotomized by lust.

It was like, start the music, 'cause it's time to run across the wheat field, baby!

Roberto went into bodyguard mode, shoving his chair up claustrophobically close to mine and screaming in my ear in a blatant attempt to distract me.

This didn't prevent the guitarist and me from staring at each other longingly across the beer-soaked table, and I caught the tangy scent of hostility rising from Roberto's sweat-soaked armpit as he put a possessive elbow on my shoulder.

Suddenly a teenaged runaway sitting at the table right next to ours leaned over and puked a couple of pitchers of beer all over the floor along with what looked like some partially digested midnight pizza.

"All right, dude!" shouted some other drunk guys approvingly.

"Jesus Christ!" bitched the snotty handkerchief, running for some napkins.

My beautiful rosy Rump Roast promptly picked up his chair, came around the table, and wedged himself in on the other side of me, smiling into my eyes. I ignored Roberto's hard elbow digging painfully into my collarbone.

"It's time to go home," Roberto shouted in my nearest ear, trying to yank my coat, which I was using as a cushion, out from under me.

"I don't want to go yet," I yelled over my shoulder at him.

"We're going! Come on, Evie, you have a rehearsal tomorrow. You need to get some sleep."

He stood up and glowered at me, throwing money on the table.

"Is that your manager?" asked Rump Roast, breathing into my other ear. "Come to the studio tomorrow. I want you *so bad*." He managed to catch my earring in his teeth just as Roberto hauled me bodily out of my chair.

"Ow!" I screamed, feeling for blood.

Rump Roast kept grinning at me and as Roberto dragged me mercilessly towards the door I saw my earring glinting between his adorable Chicklet teeth. Then he deliberately rolled it back on his tongue, blew me a wet, pouty kiss, and swallowed it.

Overcome, I fainted.

Okay, no I didn't.

PLAY DATES WITH FERRETS & FLAKES

Since I was new to Los Angeles and didn't know anyone, Roberto set up a couple of "play dates" for me with other young women who were supposed to squire me around to all the hotspots so I could get to know the territory.

After being pretty much alone in the house most of the time I was looking forward to having some friends.

Now, let me point out here that even though people usually think I'm kind of strange, I've never had trouble making friends, at any time, anywhere. Whether in Paris or Bombay or in the Greek Isles, even in places where I couldn't speak the language, I could always make a friend or two. So, call me crazy, but I came to believe that a friend is someone who likes you with no strings attached, gives without expecting anything back, and is there for you when you need them without any hidden motive.

Not so in L.A.

In L.A. a friend is someone who sticks around as long as you make them look good, and will only give you something in exchange for something of equal or greater value. If you don't know people who can help their career, don't waste your time throwing parties because your so-called friends won't show up.

An L.A. friend will pick you up at the airport—people in L.A. *love* to pick each other up at the airport because it makes them look busy and important—but should you find yourself needing a blood transfusion, baby, you'll be getting that blood from strangers, trust me.

Take Roberto and his best friend, Karl.

For the longest time Roberto rambled on about his best friend, Karl.

I had to meet Karl. Karl and I would just love each other. Karl this, Karl that, Karl, Karl, Karl.

"So where is this Karl?" I finally asked one day, like sixteen years later. "He must live awfully far away."

"No, he lives in Westwood," said Roberto. Westwood was like right down the street practically.

"Well, if Karl is your best friend and he lives right down the street, how come you never see each other?"

"What do you mean?" said Roberto. "We see each other all the time."

"Really? When was the last time you saw him, Roberto?"

"About three, no, four months ago," Roberto said.

"And when was the last time you talked to him?"

"About three or four months ago," Roberto said.

"So, if you see your best friend let's say, every six months or so, how often do you see your acquaintances?" I asked.

"Every day," he said. "But that's business. Karl and I don't do business together."

Did he really not realize how crazy he was?

"Why are you staring at me like that?" he finally said.

Whatever!

Off to the play dates I went.

The first one was with Carla, whom I promptly nicknamed Ferret Girl. She worked in the office at the studios where Roberto worked. I guess Roberto picked Carla because we were so close in age, because we certainly had nothing else in common.

Carla was tall, whip thin, and had a weird, slinky way of moving that reminded me of a ferret. She had thin brown hair, thin brown lips, and squinty, manic brown eyes like a ferret. The second I laid eyes on her I knew she was completely out of her mind.

Our pre-date telephone conversation went like this:
Brrrrring, brrrrrring (my phone).
"Hello?" I said.
"This is Carla."
"Hi, Carla! Are we still on for tonight?"
"Yeah."
"Um, did Roberto tell you where we live?"
"Ha! Roberto," she said cryptically. "Yeah, he told me."
"Why'd you say it like that?" I asked.
"Excuse me, but Roberto's like, a total fag."
"No, he's not," I said.
"Ha! Men," she said. There was silence. I heard the hiss and inhale of her lighting a cigarette with a match.
"Carla?" I said.
"Pick you up at seven," she said and hung up.

After what I had witnessed at the Christmas Party, which was kind of an amped up version of what went on at the studios every day, I wasn't too surprised to learn that Carla was a man-hater. I understood. After all, I knew from experience that being around that much unrestrained testosterone on a daily basis was kind of hard on a girl. But her insistence on Roberto's fagdom smacked of some personal beef, and sure enough, I found out later she had tried to get in Roberto's pants and he rejected her. When I asked him why, he said, "Sorry, I don't do rodents."

Carla picked me up at the apartment I shared with Roberto in her little white car.
I was waiting politely on the curb when she drove up, expecting to invite her in for a moment.
"Get in the car," was all she said, not even bothering to say hello.
We drove in silence to a contemporary, too-bright bar somewhere in North Hollywood.
During the drive through Hollywood and over the hills into the Valley, my feeble attempts at small talk were ignored or responded to with vapid monosyllables.

Carla checked her manicure at every stoplight. When we were stuck in traffic she examined her face in the rearview mirror and watched herself smoking while I picked at the calluses I had on my own ragged fingertips from years of playing the piano.

When we arrived at the bar, Carla ripped her keys out of the ignition, slammed out of the car and clipped off across the parking lot without a word. I had no choice but to follow her. Maybe her mood will improve after a drink or two, I thought optimistically.

Nope.

She ordered a 7-Up with Captain Morgan's, which I had never heard of.

"What is it?" I asked.

"Spiced rum," she said dully, glaring at some guys across the room who had watched us come in and were still staring.

"I'll have the same," I told the waiter.

Our drinks were brought, and we sipped them in silence. Further attempts to illicit important Hollywood information or just have a little girly chitchat were fruitless.

It was very uncomfortable.

I caught the guys across the room smiling at me, so I smiled back and raised my glass.

One of them clearly took my gesture as an invitation and came over to our table. He had just stretched out a hand and was opening his mouth in a greeting when Carla whipped her head around and spat on him.

"Fuck off!" she snarled, wiping 7-Up and Captain Morgan's from her chin.

"Oh god! I'm so sorry!" I said to the poor guy, who was as shocked as I was. He left in a huff.

"Why did you do that?" I asked Carla. She turned on me.

"Did you smile at them? Let me tell you something, since you're obviously totally *green*. Never smile at a guy in this town. They're all assholes. They act like all they care about is pussy, but I'm tellin' ya, they're all total fags."

"Oh. But Roberto's not like that," I said hopefully. "He's really nice!"

"Roberto's an idiot and so are you," Carla said. "Wait and see. He's only shacking up with you because the Shrimp is going to produce your record."

"He is?"

"Everybody knows."

"Everybody knows what, the shacking up or the Shrimp thing?"

"Both," she said. She set her glass down with a click. "Let's go. I gotta stop by my apartment. It's around the corner. I gotta make sure my stupid boyfriend fed my pets."

"Did you want to go somewhere else after that?" I asked, trying to sound chirpy and friendly.

"No. I gotta work tomorrow."

"Okay," I said.

"Gotta pee," she said.

When Carla slithered off to the ladies' room I ran over to the guys across the room and apologized for Carla.

"That was terrible, I'm so sorry, I don't even know her," I said.

"That's okay, sugar. We'll forgive you because you've got such great tits!" they told me.

"Hey, give us your phone number! No! Stay here with us! Got a boyfriend?"

"Well, bye then!" I said brightly.

They say that over time people come to resemble their pets. I am convinced that this is true. For years my sister reminded me of a hamster. Then she got a hedgehog, and we didn't speak to each other until she finally got a dog and became friendly again.

Guess what Carla's pets were? Yep. Ferrets!

A strong, feral musk blasted into the hallway as the apartment door swung open. Carla switched on a lamp and I saw the source—the walls were lined with cages, each containing a hissing brown ferret.

Careful to protect her own feisty claws, she opened the cages and I stood as still as possible, barely breathing, while the ferrets scampered and slithered around the room alarmingly.

"They're a lot like cats," she commented in that dull voice of hers.

Well, I may not know much about ferrets, but I have a lot of experience with cats, and believe me, these ferrets had nothing in common with any cat I have ever known.

But then, Carla thought every man who rejected her was a fag. I wondered what her "stupid boyfriend" was like. I imagined him to be like a weasel or maybe an opossum. Something pointy, nocturnal, and mean, anyway. A bat?

Carla let the ferrets zip and slink around the apartment while she placed food in the cages. Then she hissed at them and they scrambled like desperate, brainless maniacs back into their little prisons. I hastened out into the hallway to wait for her.

"Erik Estrada lives in this building, too, you know," Carla said, plunging the ferrets into darkness and locking the door behind us.

I guess I wasn't suitably impressed, because she gave an exasperated sigh.

"Get in the car," she ordered.

My next "date" was with a gorgeous redhead with a gorgeous voice who sang around town, and for some reason I want to call her "Spamalope," like that imaginary meat creature from *The Far Side* comic, but I can't really get away with that.

So let's just say her name was Debbie.

It took a while to set up the date, because Debbie never returned my calls. After leaving, like, seven messages over a period of a couple of weeks, I finally called Roberto at the studio and complained.

"Oh, don't worry about it. You're new here and she's never heard of you, so she thinks you're a nobody. Plus you're a girl and also a singer, so you're competition. Let me handle it," said Roberto.

Of course, Debbie called *Roberto* back immediately and agreed to have dinner with me in exchange for some free studio time.

"That seems kind of conniving and mercenary," I told Roberto.

"Not really," he said. "A lot of stuff happens in this town because of favors. Debbie's doing me a favor by taking you out, so I give her some studio time, return the favor. A little of her time for a little of my time."

"And what about *my* time?" I asked. "What am I getting out of this?"

"Look, Evie, I'm trying to help you out here. You need to get out and meet people. Besides, you get all the studio time you want because everybody at the studio loves you and you're working with me. I'm just giving her some studio time. It's not like I'm giving her a *gig* or anything. Just go and have a nice dinner. At least you're getting out of the house."

My experience with Ferret Girl had made me cautious, so this time I borrowed Roberto's car and drove myself to the location so I could leave if things got unpleasant. Debbie and I were supposed to meet at Genghis Cohen on Fairfax, which is a Jewish Chinese restaurant, if you can get your head around that. A smallish side room with a stage serves as a performance venue for L.A.'s working musicians. It's a good place for an artist to see and be seen, which was why Debbie wanted to go there.

I waited at our reserved table for about forty-five minutes before Debbie arrived. I waved to her and she sat down and immediately began checking her flawless face in a compact mirror.

Debbie had a big personality to go with her big voice, which I got to hear a lot of because she only stopped singing and humming to complain about her fat legs, which weren't, and tell me about her ambition, which was basically to take over the world.

I never really got a word in edgewise, but Debbie's loud, name-dropping monologue was pretty entertaining, plus she knew every other person who came in the door and had something vitally important to discuss with each and every one of them.

I barely existed on her radar.

Apparently, Debbie herself didn't exist unless someone was looking at her, because her head kept swiveling all over the place to make sure somebody was (I didn't count, being a nobody) and if nobody was (me), she looked at herself in her compact mirror until someone else relieved her of the job.

Debbie may have been pathologically self-obsessed, but she was clearly a networking professional and I decided to learn as much as I could from watching her operate. When she finally focused her attention on me, it was like being snapped in the face with a hot rubber band.

"So Evie, how come it took so long to meet you?" she said accusingly. "Roberto says you just got to town, so you can't be that busy."

Huh?

"I called you about seven times," I said. "Didn't you get my messages?"

"Oh, I get a thousand messages a day," she said importantly, cramming her mouth with Chinese Chicken Salad. "So what are you saying, I never called you back?"

"Well, no, I mean yes. You didn't," I said, confused.

"So you're calling me a flake. Are you calling me a flake?" Debbie said loudly, thus ensuring at least another five minutes of attention from the various diners at surrounding tables.

Well, the only "flakes" I knew of were made of corn or chocolate, so this was clearly yet another strange L.A. slang word, the meaning of which I was unaware of.

"What's a flake?" I asked.

"You *are* calling me a flake! And pretending you're not. God, how rude can you get. I just think that's really rude," she said.

"What's a flake, Debbie? I don't know what that means!"

"A flake is someone who never calls you back! Who makes promises and breaks them! Who doesn't show up on time!"

"Uh, Debbie, you never called me back."

"And I guess now you're going to say that I was late for our meeting, too," she said, really pissed now.

"No, I wasn't going to *say* that," I said, getting mad myself.

"Oh! You weren't going to *say* that. But you were thinking it!"

"Maybe I should go home now," I said.

"That's it, make me feel like shit and run away. You're just like all the rest."

"But," I said.

"I told Roberto I would set you up with some connections, but I don't know if I can help someone with such a bad attitude."

"But," I said.

"You really need to get your shit together, Evie, or you're not going to make it in this town."

"But," I said.

"Yeah, well, *nice* meeting you, Evie. Good luck. This was such a waste of my time."

She threw some money on the table and stood up with a dramatic flourish, looked around to make sure she had everyone's attention, and ran out the door like the Spamalope she was.

I decided I didn't need any friends.

MUSIC BUSINESS, L.A. STYLE

In between rehearsals with my band, writing new songs, and recording in the studio, Roberto and I went to business meetings with members of a surprisingly un-evolved species whose existence I had heretofore been unaware of, which were called Record Company Executives.

Now, you have to understand that everything I ever wanted had pretty much been served to me on a silver platter up to this point, so suddenly finding myself in the position of having to sell myself to these crude mud creatures came as a shock.

In my hometown and other parts of the world I had stood out as not ordinary, possibly even somewhat freakish, but accepted and appreciated as the artist I am.

Now I was in a town where even the lowliest weirdo on Hollywood Boulevard is good-looking, talented, and has something to sell.

I heard stories, many of which sounded to me like the music business version of urban myths like mice fried up as chicken, thumbs found in restaurant salads, that sort of thing.

One story going around was about a band that only got signed when they crashed into the lobby of a record company and held everyone in the reception area hostage until a Vice President gave them the contract they wanted. After that, they became the label's biggest seller of all time!

I'd made a good enough living in Europe. Weren't my songs strong enough? Surely I wouldn't have to resort to buying an Uzi.

I heard another story about a great but unattractive singer. She was apparently pushed over the edge by rejection after rejection, all based on her looks, and somehow got into a label president's office, jumped up on the desk and peed all over it while he was talking on the phone. I guess he thought that was pretty titillating because according to the story, he put his caller on the speaker phone and continued his conversation until the singer grabbed his gold records off the wall and started smashing them over his head.

She got her contract, and became the label's biggest seller of all time!

I had to ask my sweet-tempered, pacifist self: Am I capable of that?

I asked questions.

You need a lawyer. But watch it, they're sharks!

You need a manager. But watch it! They're cannibals!

I didn't want to believe any of this stuff, but it certainly seemed that in a strange town like this where everybody thinks they're special, you can't just *be* special, you have to shove it down their throats with a sharp stick and set it on fire.

Well, I didn't have any sharpened sticks, but I did have great demos.

And I hadn't yet acquired any cannibals, so I had to settle for Roberto.

We did the best we could.

Roberto took me to a glass and steel tower where we visited the offices of a hyperactive, ambulatory toadstool who was too coked up to even listen to my music but crafty enough to disguise his stupidity by making me think it was my fault.

The creeping fungus, I mean executive, listened to maybe two verses of a song and then shut it off, slurping on his cigar and staring at me through the smoke.

"Roberto was right. Your stuff is *original* and *sophisticated*. It'll never sell."

"But that's exactly why we think it *will* sell," I said.

"That's what all you idiots say. Songwriters! What is this song about?" he demanded.

"Well, if you'll listen to the song you'll…"

"Just tell me in your own words." Then before I could reply he snapped, "What inspires you? Who are your influences?"

"If you listen to the song you'll…"

"I've got a great idea!" the exec said, "You go home and think about who your top ten favorite artists are, no, make it twenty, and when you've got a list, come back and see me again."

"We just drove all the way over here and you're not even going to listen to one song? Why are we here? Why did we have this meeting?" I wanted to know.

"Hey, I'm just trying to help you, kid. If you don't even know your influences, how could you have a song for me to hear? This is the music business. Don't waste my time. Go home and make a list, like I told ya." He gnawed on his soggy cigar.

I was dumbfounded. I looked at Roberto, expecting him to say something in my defense, but he chose this moment to abandon salesmanship for ass-kissing, the obsequious bastard.

"Good idea, sir! Thank you for your time," said my so-called friend, the wimp.

Can you tell I was a little unhappy with this?

"Make a list?" I shouted at him in the elevator.

"Hush, wait until we get outside," Roberto said.

"What does making lists have to do with anything?" I asked Roberto when we were in the car heading to our next meeting. "He didn't even listen to my songs!"

"Yeah, he was a prick," said Roberto. "Don't worry about it. I know this next guy personally. But you might want to think about who your favorite artists are in case it comes up again."

I thought this was the dumbest thing I'd ever heard and I said so.

"You've got to play the game, Evie," Roberto told me. "These guys are idiots. They know nothing about music. They're pencil pushers and they're stupid and they suck, but they are the ones behind the desk, they hold the contracts, they have the power. You could try speaking up a little more. They see you sitting there and all they see is a babe with big blue eyes and major tits—"

"Roberto!"

"Hey, I'm just telling you how it is, Evie, don't get mad at me. This is Hollywood! Yeah, if they listened to your songs they'd get you right away. But we have to make them *want* to hear your songs. Maybe you shouldn't leave all the talking up to me is all I'm saying."

"But I don't know what to say to them," I said, frustrated. "If they listened to the music, I would know what to say, but if they don't even listen to the music—hello? We're having a meeting about music? You have to listen to it—then what is there to talk about?"

"You're right! You're right! Okay, look, just try to open up a little, give them an idea who you are, okay? I'm doing my best."

This was unfortunately true.

But maybe he was right. Clearly Roberto didn't have nearly the clout he'd led me to believe he had. He was turning out to be a major disappointment. This meant it was all up to me, as usual.

So I tried to help out more.

When the next exec asked me the same question about influences, I rattled off some names. "Queen, Gentle Giant, Kate Bush, Beethoven, Chopin," I said.

"Never heard of 'em," he said.

"Bon Jovi?" I said, fishing. "Guns N Roses, Pat Benatar? Devo? Men at Work?"

"Buncha old farts. Where ya been?" He tapped his desk with a polished, instructive finger. "You need to start listening to current bands, girlie. Maybe move to Seattle. All the hot bands are coming from there now. Yeah, that's it, move to Seattle and write some real songs and come back when you're done."

Your turn, Roberto! I pinched his thigh.

Roberto tried.

"Uh, Evie's not your, like, garage band. She does rock, but she's a pianist, classically trained," ventured Roberto. "Plus she's traveled a lot. You have to understand the universal appeal of her music. She has a lot of influences."

"Oh, I see," said the exec. "Piano players! Too sophisticated for this market. You've got your Tori Amos, but she has a gimmick. Redhead who humps her piano bench. You do that? No? You should think about it. The guys would get off on a stacked blonde like you humping the bench."

I glared at him with my eyes narrowed until he got embarrassed.

"Okay, shit. Let's see your lyrics."

I gave him some of my best lyrics, neatly typed on good paper.

"What's this, a goddamn resume? Christ, it's an essay!" he laughed. "Who's gonna read all these *words*?"

"What do you mean? It's a song that tells a story!" I said.

"Yeah, yeah, a story," the guy said, derisively waving my lyrics around by the tips of his fingers.

"What you got to understand is the average American isn't listening to the *words*. You can't be trying to reach people with a sixth grade education with all these *words*. You can't woo them with *language* when they can barely put a sentence together. You have to hit them over the head with a sledge hammer! Bam! Bam! Bam!"

"Excuse me? Sir?" said Roberto, finally speaking up. "Evie's a poet. She's into the *craft* of song writing, like Joni Mitchell, or Leonard Cohen, or Dylan."

The guy's face turned bright red and I saw a vein start throbbing in his temple.

"How can you say that!" he shouted. "Nobody's like Dylan! Bob Dylan is God! You're comparing this bug-eyed little bimbo to *him?*"

"Hey! Why don't you listen to the tape and get back to us?" suggested Roberto.

"Oh sure! You think I have time for this crap? I'm a busy guy! Know where this belongs?"

Wham! My tape hit the trash can. "Comparing a piano-humper to Dylan. Christ!"

"How dare you!" I yelled.

I stood up, and I guess Roberto saw that I was about to lunge across the desk and punch his lights out, because in one amazingly swift movement he grabbed my lyrics and my briefcase and muscled me out of the room.

"You should have let me punch his lights out, Roberto! He probably would have signed me!"

"Forget all this crap," said Roberto. "Let's go to the beach. Fucking creep."

I wept all the way down Sunset Boulevard, through West Hollywood and Beverly Hills. By the time we reached the Pacific Coast Highway I had calmed down and was just staring out the window, sniffing occasionally.

"Evie, I'm really sorry about this. I don't know what to say," said Roberto miserably. "I brought you back here from England and I am 100% responsible for putting you through this."

Well, I wasn't about to deny that my current misery was his entire fault. *Why should I try to make him feel better?* I sulked.

"Hey," he tried again. "Those guys were bastards, okay? You'll get a deal. You got a deal in London."

"Yeah! And I didn't even have to try! I just played, and people showed up and offered me stuff! Nobody asked about my 'influences.' This is crazy! It doesn't make any sense!"

"But this is different. This is Los Angeles. Things are tougher here. But you'll make it, Evie. I believe in you. Hey, The Beatles got turned down by every label before they got signed, remember?"

Well, at least Roberto believed in me, and even if he was an ass-kisser, I knew he had good taste.

"You're right," I finally said. "Can we not talk about this anymore please? I have a headache."

We decided to drive up to Neptune's Net.

Neptune's Net is a little surfer shack on the coast where you can sit outside at picnic tables in your bare feet, watching the sun set over the waves, which is what we did, over plates of crabs we had picked out of a tank, steaming corn on the cob, and a couple of pitchers of beer. This was a weekday, so the only other customers were some totally California blonde guys with deep tans who went inside to order after jamming their surfboards upright into the sand. Pretty soon they came back out and sat down, tossing their long, sun-bleached hair around and flashing perfect teeth when they laughed.

I tried to control my staring, knowing how it pissed Roberto off. But

I couldn't help it. Having spent years among cold, overdressed northerners with scurvy and discolored teeth I was still amazed by the gorgeous, nearly naked guys I got to look at every day here in Southern California.

Then somebody even more interesting came onto the porch.

A big guy came in, followed by a woman in large, dark sunglasses, very pale and terribly thin, cradling something in her arms like a baby. Except it wasn't a baby, it was a large iguana.

I nudged Roberto, who looked over and started giggling. The woman glared at him and sat down, crooning to her big lizard. Her companion disappeared inside and came back with a pitcher of beer and a couple of glasses. A few minutes later he went to pick up their order, and I watched, fascinated, as the woman peeled boiled shrimp and fed them to the reptile from her own mouth.

"Now I've seen everything," I said.

"No you haven't," said Roberto.

CUPCAKE

We decided to abandon our educational but pointless and irritating forays into the Houses of the Holy Music Business for the time being, because the Shrimp finally finished with Mariah or Cher or somebody and said he was ready to work with me.

"You have a much better chance at getting a deal through somebody like Shrimp," Roberto told me, finally being honest now that his hotshot L.A. guy cover was blown.

The Shrimp and Cupcake lived in a big house in the Hills, and in this house the Shrimp had a secret recording studio tucked away in a small locked room hidden behind a large screen TV, which was the only furniture besides an old beat up couch.

"Did you guys just move in?" I asked Cupcake.

"No, why?"

"Because you don't have any furniture."

"Yes, we do. We have this couch."

"Oh."

When I asked why he had to hide his equipment behind a locked door, the Shrimp explained that certain commercial studio owners were ganging up to prevent people from disrupting the "good-ol'-boy" style music business by making records on their own. Some of these people came up to his house from time to time, and obviously he didn't want the industry to find out what he, one of it's favorite good-ole-boy producers, was up to behind it's back.

There was another reason the Shrimp kept his gear locked up, but he didn't tell me about that right off the bat.

So I started working with the Shrimp. We got together up at his house a couple of times a week and things started coming together pretty quickly, although I seemed to be doing an awful lot of the producing and he was mostly knob-twiddling. I didn't care. I was just happy to be getting something done for a change.

Well, the more time you spend with people, the more comfortable they get, and pretty soon they're letting things slip and next thing you know they're doing their private little freaky things right in front of you to see how far they can go.

The first few weeks went by normally enough. Then one day Cupcake came to the door and let me in, which was odd, because she hardly ever left their bedroom.

"Where's Shrimp?" I asked.

"He's in the kitchen," she said grimly.

I knew the Shrimp never cooked or anything like that. "What's he doing?" I asked.

She just rolled her eyes and disappeared upstairs.

As I crossed the vast, empty living room, headed towards the kitchen, I heard the sound of the microwave door closing and the beep of the buttons as the timer was set.

I opened my mouth to say, "Hey, Shrimp!"

BOOM! *Tinkle tinkle tinkle.*

"Ha, ha ha!" the Shrimp shouted gleefully. "That was so great! Evie, come in here and watch this."

He had a pile of light bulbs on the counter top. He opened the microwave door and I saw it was full of broken glass.

"What are you doing?" I said nervously. "You're not supposed to put metal in there!"

"I know! Watch this! This is so cool. Get ready to duck!" He put another light bulb in the microwave and turned it on.

I have to admit the miniature lightening storm inside the bulb was really pretty, before the light bulb exploded with a muffled BOOM! And the microwave oven jumped about a foot in the air. We threw ourselves on the floor. The microwave fizzled and started to smoke.

"Oh, man! Wasn't that the coolest? I know you're not supposed to do that," said Shrimp, giggling and wiping his eyes. "I've gone through five microwaves this month. Cupcake is really steamed about it. But she made me promise to stop pissing off the neighbors and not build anymore bombs in the garage, so…"

Cupcake's extreme tension was beginning to make sense. She was married to a homicidal maniac.

"What did you do to the neighbors?" I asked, not sure I wanted to know.

"Well, they were complaining about the loud music coming from up here? So I got one of them big spotlights and put it on the roof and aimed it right at their bedroom window? Then I rigged up the sound system to blast right at their house and played German music and Hitler's speeches at them all night. They're Jewish."

"Um, aren't you Jewish, too?" I said.

"Yeah. So? Don't you think that's funny?"

I decided not to ask what he had been doing with the bombs.

"How come you guys don't have a maid?" I asked one day, when I saw Cupcake sweeping the kitchen floor herself.

"Look around," said Cupcake. "There's nothing to clean."

"So…did Shrimp stop blowing stuff up in the microwave?"

"Yeah, he finally got bored with that. But now we're in trouble with the neighbors again." She gave a dry, rueful laugh.

"Why? What did he do?"

"They bought this boy and he cries all the time."

"*Bought this boy?*" I said.

"Adopted him. So he cries all the time and Shrimp got tired of it so he set mousetraps all over their front steps and when the woman came out with the baby in the stroller…you know how you have to go down the steps backwards…"

"Oh my god!"

"Yeah. I guess she's got a couple of broken toes." Cupcake stared at the floor for a minute, grinding her teeth.

All that aside, the work went well, and before long we had the basic rhythm tracks recorded, an outline of a drum pattern and the piano, bass, guitars, and guide vocals. We were just starting to fool around with the strings one afternoon, having a great time, when suddenly Cupcake started screaming upstairs. I stared at the Shrimp, expecting him to do something, but he just smiled at me and looked kind of sheepish.

"Aaaah! AAAAhhhhh!" went Cupcake, then broke into hysterical sobs. *CRASH! BANG!*

It sounded like she was breaking furniture up there.

"Shrimp! What's the matter with Cupcake?"

"Oh, don't worry. She does this every so often. She'll stop soon," he said, a little nervously. "She just gets a little upset sometimes. Maybe you should leave."

Suddenly Cupcake went quiet. We stared at each other, listening. Then we heard Cupcake hurtling down the stairs.

"Uh oh," said the Shrimp.

Cupcake yanked the studio door open. Mascara was smeared down her cheeks and she was holding a baseball bat.

"Hi, honey!" said the Shrimp, like she had just come in with the tea or something.

"Get out of here, Evie!" she screeched at me. "Just get out!"

"Cupcake," I said.

"I said get out! Do you hear me, get out of this house or I'll burn your tapes! Get out of my way! I'm going to break everything in this room, Shrimp! I swear to God! Aaaaaa!"

"Let's go," the Shrimp said to me.

I grabbed my stuff and ran past Cupcake, who, for some reason, let me pass and even let the Shrimp lock the studio door behind him, though she didn't stop yelling.

"Fuckers! You goddamn fuckers!"

We ran out the front door and jumped into his Mercedes as Cupcake started tearing the kitchen apart, ripping doors off the cupboards and smashing the refrigerator, screaming obscenities.

The Shrimp took me to a Thai restaurant.
I sat across from him, twitching over a bowl of soup.
"Will she really burn our tapes?" I asked.
"No, ha, ha ha! She wouldn't do that," he said, but I noticed he was biting his lips and sweating. "But we should probably stop working together for a while."
He forked up some Pad Thai.
"So, now you know why we don't have any furniture," he said. "Every time I buy some, she breaks it, so I stopped buying any. That couch is practically indestructible, ha!"
"Should I be worried about this? I don't really know how to handle it, Shrimp."
"Oh, don't worry. There's nothing you can do. Just lie low for a few weeks. Hopefully she'll leave you alone."
"Leave *me* alone? *Me?* But I didn't do anything!"
"No, but neither did my last secretary. She quit because Cupcake made her life hell for a while. So far she's left the new one alone. Before that she terrorized my manager. I had to change firms. Cupcake doesn't know where the office is."
"Can't you take her to a doctor, a shrink or something?"
"Oh, no, she would never go…she's okay! Everybody gets a little crazy sometimes, heh heh! It's best if you just stay out of her way. Don't call the house or anything."
I couldn't eat. My stomach felt like a rock.
"When will we be able to work together again?" I asked.
"Uh, I don't know…the last artist I tried to produce killed himself."
"Because of *Cupcake?*"
"Yeah. You gonna eat that soup?"

At six o'clock the next morning the phone rang.
"Hello?" I said groggily.

"*You killed my dog!*" Cupcake yelled.

"Cupcake? You don't have a dog," I said.

"I had a dog! You killed it! Where's my book on Tibet? You killed my *book* and stole my *dog*, you little bitch!"

I just stared at the phone, incredulous. This was a whole new kind of crazy. I didn't know what to say.

"Do you know what time it is?" she screeched. "Don't you ever call me at six o'clock in the morning again!"

"Cupcake, you called me! What are you talking about? What dog? What book?"

"I burned your tapes," she hissed malevolently. "I burned them up, you little cow. And you might as well go back to Europe, you thief! You *MURDERER!* And don't bother trying to get a deal in this town. This is MY town. I OWN these people! I've sent faxes to every studio, every record company! With your picture! Everybody knows what a creep you are! *GO TO HELLLLLLLLL!*"

She hung up.

I thought maybe the Shrimp would call to tell me what was going on. I waited a couple of hours, but Shrimp didn't call. So I called the studio and asked the owner if he was there.

"Yes, but to tell you the truth, Evie, you better not come over here anymore for a while. Cupcake is trying to blacklist you."

"What?" This was unbelievable. "But I haven't done anything!"

"I know, I know. Everybody knows. Cupcake is insane. But I can't help you. They're important clients of mine. I can't afford to have the Shrimp take his projects somewhere else."

I called the Shrimp's manager and got pretty much the same speech.

"I'm his manager," said his manager. "How do you think it would look if I took your side, even though you're right? In the big picture, you don't mean anything, sweetheart."

I thought I at least had Roberto as an ally. But he worked at the studio, often with the Shrimp. Guess whose side he took, the sniveling bootlicker?

"Sorry about all this, but I can't afford to lose my job. My reputation is at stake here."

"Roberto! I left everything I had going on in England because you said things would be good for me here! You're my only friend! You can't just drop me now, because of some crazy bitch!"

"Yes, I can. Sorry," said Roberto. "Guess you're just not cut out for the big time. Pack your stuff and be out of the apartment by the time I come home."

So there I was, abandoned in Hollywood, with no money to go back to Europe, no friends, no way to continue the work I had begun with the Shrimp.

I still had most of a band, but they weren't any help, since they were either living with their parents or in some squalid antique Hollywood dump full of Nigerian dope addicts and carnival rejects.

I cancelled all our gigs, afraid Cupcake would see the ads in the papers and show up with her baseball bat to smash my piano in front of my handful of loyal fans.

Damned if I was going to ask Aunt Jet and Hellcat for assistance.

No matter which way I turned, I was staring at a blank wall. I felt trapped.

Plus the whole thing was totally embarrassing.

So I took the only option left open to me, and faked my own death. Okay, no I didn't.

I packed up my stuff and with the help of my three hardcore fans, moved into a small bungalow in the hills above Echo Park, which is a neighborhood at the unfashionable east end of Sunset Boulevard.

I've heard they've fixed it up now since the real estate scammers have run out of people to gouge on the West Side, but back then Echo Park was more or less a ghetto. There were a lot of gang-related fires and shootings.

My car was broken into practically every night by a particularly nasty gang of foul-mouthed six-year-olds who lived across the street. They even managed to hotwire it one night, but since none of them were tall enough to see over the dashboard, let alone manipulate the pedals, it was still idling on the street when I went out the next day.

I thought it would be fun to rent a paddle boat and tool around on the lake amidst the water lilies, but changed my mind when the guy who owns the boats told me the lake was full of corpses the cops didn't want anyone to find.

As if there wasn't enough going on to keep me on my toes, helicopters flew low over the neighborhood at night, shining searchlights through the rattling windows. I figured they were looking for outlaws and refugees, but evidently they were spraying something as well, because every time the helicopters showed up, the next morning my car was covered with something sticky and gritty that seemed to be eating its way through my windshield.

I asked the Mexican mailman about it.

"Med fly spray," said the mailman.

"What's a med fly?" I asked.

"It's a kind of fruit fly. They say they spray this chemical to kill them, but ha, ha, there's no fruit flies."

I had to give this some thought. There had to be some bigger plan, and finally I figured it out.

I have a number of conspiracy theories. For one thing, I'm convinced that the American Dental Association is in cahoots with the people who package dried beans. If you've ever cooked your own beans, you'll know that every bag of beans contains about a thousand pebbles that look exactly like the beans.

Chances are you're like me, too busy or lazy to sort the beans properly, so you just chuck 'em all in the pot. And chances are you read or watch TV while you eat, chomping along when crack! Bye-bye molar.

They must have a bunch of guys who get paid by the hour to find pebbles that look like beans.

So, if my theories about the nefarious activities of government agencies are correct, it makes sense to me that in Los Angeles, where many kinds of fruit trees grow in abundance, they would poison the wonderful, healthy plants that grow naturally in the area so that you are forced to go to the grocery store to buy horrible, imported produce from Chile or wherever, old fruit and vegetables that have been waxed and dyed and injected with things in order to make them look new and fresh and normal.

Besides this practice helping to keep the grocery stores in business, there is the added economic benefit of people getting malnutrition from eating dead food, so they have to buy more and more food to get the nutrients they need.

So people think they're taking care of themselves because they are eating pounds of store-bought fruit and vegetables, but they are actually getting sicker and fatter, because that's what happens with long-term malnutrition. If your body thinks it's starving, it will hold on to whatever you put in it as long as possible to keep you alive.

In the old days one well-grown, carefully nurtured turnip could keep, say, six people alive for a week. Now those six people have to eat a truckload of turnips a day to get the same nutrients. Who has time to chop all those vegetables? It's easier and cheaper just to go to McDonald's.

But then you'll pay through the nose for vitamins and a weight loss program that doesn't work because chances are you have some crappy low paying desk job and can't afford a gym membership.

They get away with this by claiming there's a terrible plague of Mediterranean fruit flies in L.A. eating all the fruit. Hello! Am I the only one paying attention? We don't need to import fruit from South America! Who do they think they're kidding?

People, there are no Mediterranean fruit flies in Los Angeles. Mediterranean fruit flies live in the Mediterranean! Clearly they just want to scare people into shopping at the grocery store.

I've lived all over Los Angeles and I can tell you firsthand that I have never seen one single fruit fly that didn't come out of a box of imported bananas, pal.

What they are *really* doing is spraying a mind control chemical on everyone, something that makes people stupid, angry, and fat, and also makes them crave Starbucks.

Okay, okay, I'll shut up about that now.

Anyway, I hid there in Echo Park for a while, paranoid that Cupcake would somehow find me and send a hit man or something. God only knew what someone that crazy was capable of.

When she didn't call and nobody showed up to blow my brains out, I ventured out to take walks, but progress was slow because I was as jumpy as a cat, compulsively checking behind every tree and bush to make sure Cupcake wasn't lurking, ready to jump out at any moment, screaming "*MURDERER!*"

I bit my nails and succumbed to regular panic attacks. I was sure I had an ulcer.

I woke myself up yelling in the night. My neighbors avoided me in the street.

I drank so much wine the guys in the liquor store started to make fun of me.

Obviously I didn't have a job, or I wouldn't be at the liquor store every other day. But I didn't look like a street person either. José decided I had to be some crazy rich broad with delusions of grandeur, or a failed actress who had lost her mind.

"You gonna jump off the Hollywood sign like that other chick, right? You call me when you do it, right? I wanna see that."

"Si, let us know when you gonna jump senorita, ha!"

They started referring to me as the Queen of Echo Park.

Pretty soon when I showed up at the liquor store every morning or so, a small crowd of brown people were there to wave and cheer for me.

"Queen of Echo Park! Wave at us! We bow to you, the Queen of Echo Park."

They picked Nasturtium blossoms off the bushes in the parking lot and threw them at my car in a mockery of adulation.

One day I decided to act really crazy, grabbed a handful of the flowers and stuffed them in my mouth. This is how I discovered that Nasturtiums are really tasty! They are especially good tossed in a salad with arugula and a light balsamic vinaigrette, just so you know.

Eventually I realized that by succumbing to alcoholic depression, I had let Cupcake win. I had no friends, no career. I was completely alone.

Then one day I woke up, the birds were singing in the avocado trees, the brilliant California sun was streaming in the window, and for once the voices in my head were silent.

Wait a minute, I thought. *Now who's acting crazy?*

I still had my life, my brains, my beauty and talent, two albums, and seven hundred unrecorded songs. No one could take that from me. Besides, why was I mourning the loss of those assholes?

I'd start all over. Screw them!

CAPTAIN BOB AND WHITE BUFFALO SPIRIT

They say that when you let go of the past and open your heart to new experiences, the Universe does cool stuff for you.

So I did, and sure enough, one day something amazing happened.

I was on the freeway, zooming along in my car, when I noticed a big white truck was keeping pace with me in the next lane. You don't drive right next to someone on a Los Angeles freeway unless you want to get shot. Everybody knows that!

But this guy wasn't moving ahead or falling behind, so finally I looked at him.

He was a tall brown man with long black hair, and he was gesturing frantically at me to pull over.

Was something wrong with one of my tires? Was my skirt caught in the door? Had my registration tags been stolen again?

I tried slowing down, and he slowed down. I sped up, and he kept pace with me, waving his arm and pointing to the right. Pull over! Pull over!

He wouldn't give up, so finally I indicated I was going to take the next exit, and he followed me.

We pulled into the parking lot of a Hamburger Hamlet. I got out of the car warily, fisting my keys in case I needed to gouge his eyes out.

"Whew, I thought you would never stop! I must have been following you for at least five miles," said the guy.

He was about seven feet tall, sinewy, and looked like a Native American. He was wearing sweat pants and a "wife-beater," which is one of those sweatshirts with the arms cut off that I guess guys wear to look tough when they beat their wives or something.

"What do you want?" I said.

"This will probably sound strange to you, but when you passed me on the freeway I saw that you had some questions and I might be able to answer them."

Okay, that sounded a little strange, but hey, I'm a friend of the exorcist, right?

But he didn't seem dangerous, even though he was big and obviously strong. His voice was mellow and gentle. Plus he looked like an Indian, and I've always had a fondness for native people, being part Cherokee myself.

He looked pointedly at my hand, bristling aggressively with keys. I dropped my keys in my purse. He stepped forward then, and smiled. His teeth were very white.

"People call me Captain Bob," he said. "And you are the one I was sent to find."

Oh, shit! Was this Cupcake's hit man? How did she find me?

He laughed and reached for my hand, which looked like a little defenseless white clam when enclosed in his long brown fingers.

"I know many things about you. Allow me to introduce myself. I am a Medicine Man of the Sierra Madre Apache, and friend of White Buffalo," he intoned solemnly. "The Star People of your tribe keep watch over their singers. They know when one is being led astray."

It was kind of surreal to hear this standing in the parking lot of Hamburger Hamlet with traffic whizzing by. I mean, it wasn't like I'd gone on some random freaky vision quest looking for a sign. There were a couple of hookers arguing on the corner, for Christ's sake.

"Let's go in here and get an iced tea, Cherokee Star Singer," said Captain Bob.

I hesitated.

"Are you afraid?" he asked, his big dark eyes full of gentle humor.

"No," I lied.

Captain Bob laughed again, low and sweet.

"Good, there's no reason to be afraid. The Universe has heard your cry for help. I was sent to be your guide."

Okay! I thought. Nutcase or not, anyway the guy was cute in a big Indian, tall-enough-to-be-a-giraffe kind of way.

Over several glasses of iced tea I told Captain Bob my story so far. He laughed his head off, like, every five minutes, which pissed me off at first but then I found to my surprise that I was laughing, too. We laughed and laughed and laughed, wiping our eyes on our napkins.

"Oh, you will have to write a book about this some day. It will be a best-seller, I'm sure of it!"

Hey folks! Was he psychic or what?

"So, what are you going to do now?" he asked.

"Well, that's my question, if I have one," I said. "What do I do now?"

"There is a small band of Sioux living here quietly. Their ceremonies are the only reason the evil, ridiculous city of Los Angeles has not been buried by the mountains or swallowed by the sea. I will take you to them, Star Singer. They will help you find your destiny. But first you must purify yourself and prepare prayers for the sweat lodge. Then the spirits will hear you and come to your aid."

Wow! Indians and sweat lodges and spirits! All *right*!

"Take me to your leader," I joked.

Out in the parking lot Captain Bob gave me a pouch of dried plants and some animal bones to put under my pillow for three nights. He also gave me his phone number, making me promise not to give it to anyone else. I have since forgotten it, so don't bother trying to force it out of me, okay? Learn to deal with your own problems.

Anyway, I did what Captain Bob said. I fasted, eating only the herbs from the pouch and drinking nothing but water.

I walked around barefoot singing, "Hiya-ya-ya hiya-ya-ya hi, hiya ho!" to myself and slept with bones under my pillow.

For the first time in weeks, I was actually happy.

Up yours, Cupcake! I thought. *Who cares if I'm blacklisted! I'm a Cherokee Star Singer!*

It all felt very witchy and exciting.

* * *

A few days later Captain Bob picked me up and drove me to a secret location in the Valley where the sweat lodge ceremony was going to take place.

He had told me to bring a pure cotton dress to wear in the lodge, and some loose tobacco as an offering.

The tobacco part was easy, but try to find a simple cotton garment in Los Angeles! Everything was made of spandex, Lycra, leather, acrylic and nylon, stuff designed to make bodies as yet unperfected by extensive plastic surgery to look as though they were. Finally I found one of those shapeless muumuu house dresses at Sears. It had a hellish design in garish colors, like a carpet in a third world hotel, but it was pure cotton.

Well, Captain Bob said we'd be sitting in the dark, so I figured I could overcome my vanity long enough to talk to some spirits, who probably don't care what we look like anyway.

For those of you who haven't had the privilege, a sweat lodge is a prayer and purification ceremony in which you guess what, sweat a lot, probably more than you ever have in your whole life. There's a lot more to it than praying and sweating, of course, but if you really want to know about it, make an effort.

And don't bother with any honky-ass copycat ceremony run by some white trash back-to-the-land-er who is trying to sell a book.

Ask questions. Don't be fooled. The copycats produce colorful brochures, wear a lot of silver jewelry, and are usually in cahoots with a travel agency that specializes in dude ranch vacations.

People involved with the real deal won't give, sell, or tell you anything about it.

They'll dissemble, dismiss, and even lie to you if you're too persistent. They play dumb. They act stupid. You won't get anywhere with them.

That's how you'll know you're onto something.

* * *

The actual lodge is kind of a round cage made from young willow trees covered with tarps, since it's pretty hard to get hold of buffalo skins nowadays. There is a shallow pit in the center for the heated stones, which are carried in by the fire keeper on a pair of antlers. Prayer ties made from tobacco and colored bits of cloth hang from the roof over the stones. Every element of nature is represented in the lodge. The floor is earth, the breath is air, and there is fire and water. The peoples of all nations are represented: tree people and stone people, animal and bird people, and human people.

The lodge represents the womb, and the people crawl into it on their hands and knees. Traditionally a sweat lodge ceremony is performed naked, but when can you ever rely on white men to behave themselves in mixed company? Right, never! So now people wear clothes.

"I'd better warn you. This is going to be intense," Captain Bob told me.

"Why?" I said.

"Because White Buffalo, the Elder is here. When he runs the lodge, things happen. That's why I brought you tonight."

"Intense how? Like, super hot?"

"Well, it's always hot, but you might see and hear things. Don't freak out. If you really need to get out of the lodge they will let you but you have to wait for the end of a song."

"I'm not scared," I said.

So we crawled into the lodge, someone brought the rocks, and they closed the door. There were so many people we had to sit with our knees up. There was no room to change position. My toes were hanging over the lip of the hole where the burning rocks were glowing. Other than that soft red glow, it was completely dark.

White Buffalo spoke, the people prayed and sang. Someone beat a drum. White Buffalo talked some more, told stories, the people laughed. Then they sang some more. Every so often White Buffalo poured water on the rocks, and hot steam blasted our faces. The temperature rose higher and higher.

They opened the door now and then and passed around the ladle of water, which helped a little. But I swear, you've never been so hot in your life. I mean we were *cooking*. I could feel myself shrinking as the toxins poured out of my skin.

"Now you gonna ask for what you want. Tell the spirits what you seeking for your life," said White Buffalo.

A new song started. The people sang louder and louder. I heard people gasping for air and crying and praying.

"We're gonna die," I thought.

The heat was excruciating and there was no way to get away from it. There wasn't room to lie down.

I prayed. "Help me, I can't take this," I whispered, and something strange happened.

A pale blue mist snaked out of the rocks, oozed up and over my feet and wrapped itself around me. The mist was cold!

Suddenly I realized that even though it was pitch dark in the lodge, I could not only see the mist, I could also see myself. Then I looked around and realized I could see White Buffalo, too, and he was looking right at me! And he was laughing!

"Ask for what you want!" he said, and somehow I heard him even with all the racket. "Go on, ask for what you want! Even if it's stupid! Ha, ha, ha!"

Even if it's stupid?

Okay, was this little old Indian guy making fun of me? Well screw him! I want a manager and a record deal! I prayed in my head. A manager and record deal! Manager! Record deal! Manager! Record deal!

The people were singing at the top of their lungs, banging on the drums faster and faster. Suddenly I heard a huge animal galloping around outside the lodge, and then it seemed to gallop straight through it. I heard a bird cry and giant wings beat close to my face. I felt the feathers touch my skin. Rattles were shaken around the circle. Tiny blue lights zipped this way and that, whistling shrilly as they danced around our heads.

At last the song ended. The invisible animals and the blue lights and whistles, rattles and bells vanished. Somebody opened the door and everyone went, "Ahhhhhh." As the cool air rushed in.

"All of you, you gonna get what you asked for tomorrow. Pay attention! You gonna get what you want," said White Buffalo.

Finally, we crawled out of the lodge and flopped on the grass, gasping. My muumuu was soaking wet and weighed about four hundred pounds.

When I was able to raise my head, I saw White Buffalo beckoning to me.

I hauled myself up and staggered over to where he was standing near the fire.

White Buffalo put his arms around me in a very gentle, fatherly way.

"You gotta learn what things are and what things are not," he said. "You already know a little, but you not solid in your self. What is true is in your self, not outside. You gonna get solid in your self. Not gonna be easy," he said.

Then he guffawed for about ten minutes, snorting and wiping his eyes.

"What's so funny?" I asked.

"Ah, oh, you just so hilarious! 'Manager! Record deal! Manager! Record deal!' Ha ha ha ha ha!"

How could he know that's what I asked for? I never said it out loud.

"Don't worry, not a bad thing to ask. You gonna survive. Have fun, Cherokee Star Singer."

White Buffalo had said I was going to get what I wanted, so the next day I paid attention, wondering how my new manager was going to manifest him or herself.

At first I was afraid to leave the house in case I missed something. Then I was afraid to stay home in case I missed something. Then I decided that what *I* did was irrelevant. The spirits would find a way. Sure enough, that afternoon the phone rang.

"Is this Evie London?" said a guy.

"Yes," I said.

"This is Xavier. You might not remember me, but I'm the cousin of the brother of the uncle of that guy you dated, the one with the friend?"

"Uh, yeah?"

"Well, this is pretty weird but I was going through some old stuff and found your phone number on a napkin from that restaurant we went to that one time? Which of course was an old number, but it got me thinking about how interesting you used to be and I thought I'd see if I could find you and give you a call. So what are you up to these days?"

"I'm looking for a manager and a record deal," I said.

"Really? Funny you should say that, because I was just talking to a guy yesterday who was interested in getting into artist management. I'm meeting him for dinner in Beverly Hills tonight. You want to come?"

Wow, I thought. *Those White Buffalo spirits sure don't mess around!*

Xavier, whom I vaguely remembered as being kind of an idiot, picked me up in his sleek black Mercedes at seven.

Oh, that guy! I thought when I saw him. Rich and cute, but dumb as a post. In the dog world he'd be a Labrador retriever. Pet me! Love me!

Okay, okay.

I wasn't interested in him, anyway.

Reuben Solperstein was a middle-aged former executive with a golf tan and a paunch. He was originally from New York, and Jewish, of course.

"Of course," I said. Anybody who is anybody in Los Angeles is either Jewish or the child of a movie star. Which was why, despite my superior education and worldliness and beauty and poise and grace, I was still locked out.

Lacking Jewishness and movie star parents, obviously I needed some powerful Jews to back me up. Clever spirits! Why didn't I think of that?

So Reuben lived in Palm Springs, he said, but kept a little apartment in Beverly Hills for when he came into town on business. He had an office there too, which he went to every day to wait for the phone to ring and it never did.

"So I was thinking, why not try something new? I ran a coupla production companies, dabbled in real estate, produced a couple movies, yawn, boring! Hate actors! Anyways, why not the music business?"

"Why not?" I said. "But, like, do you know the business? It's not like real estate, you know. Plus there are some real crazies in this town."

I decided not to mention that I was blacklisted.

"Don't worry about it. I know people. In fact, first thing we're gonna do is, I'm going to introduce you to a friend of mine from Palm Springs. Name's Sparky Goldstein."

"'Sparky?'" I said.

"Yeah, Sparky Goldstein. You never heard of him? He's a legend! He gave Bob Dylan his first deal. Plus all the girls he signed got famous. Olivia, Helen Reddy. He's a little older, not running a label anymore, but he's still pulling strings. Great guy. He's gonna love ya."

"Wonderful!" I said. "But don't you think you should listen to my music first, so you know what to say if he asks about it?"

"What for?" he said. "I can tell you got what it takes. You're a classy broad. I'm gonna manage you. Got a lawyer? No? Get one. Draw up your standard management contract, off we go."

How totally exciting! My dreams were about to come true.

We decided I had to do a show right away.

"You got a band?" Reuben asked.

"I can scrape some people together."

"Scrape?" he said, raising an eyebrow.

"Don't worry," I said. "All my friends are world class. Some are Grammy nominees."

I wasn't thinking of my own band, obviously. I was thinking of people I knew through the studio, musicians who would be sympathetic to what I'd gone through with Cupcake, and who would be willing to do a freebie showcase if I promised to hire them for the tour.

I got busy right away.

I found a lawyer through BMI, my performance rights society, and put him to work on the management contract. I called all the musicians I knew, who were more than happy to help, as I expected. Being a musician is a lot like being a servant. No matter how good you are, people treat you like crap and try not to pay you. So we help each other out as much as possible, if only for the chance to play some really good music, really well. That right there is its own reward, thank you very much.

Reuben sent me flowers. "To my little star," said the card. "You're gonna be famous!"

I booked a night on the stage at Genghis Cohen, the Jewish Chinese place where I'd gone to meet the Spamalope, and started rehearsing with my new superstar band.

Now all I needed was a hairdo and maybe a makeup artist.

I didn't know any. I called Reuben.

"Hey, Reuben, do you know any hairdressers?"

"Oh, yeah, the best. Guy's a wizard. Works at a place on Rodeo Drive."

"That sounds kind of expensive," I said. "I don't have much money."

"Don't worry about it. Think I can't afford to invest in my star?"

Reuben set up the appointment and gave me the address of the salon.

"What's the hairdresser's name?" I asked.

"Ask for, 'The Messiah.'"

"What?"

"He calls himself, 'The Messiah.' Ha, ha, ha! You know, like the son of God? He's a nutcase, but when someone's that good, they can call themselves whatever they want. Besides, in this town a good stylist *is* a savior. When you need new pictures, who do you call first, before the photographer?"

"Um, the stylist?"

"Right! So you know what I'm talking about."

THE MESSIAH OF
BEVERLY HILLS

The salon on Rodeo Drive was big, beautiful, and expensive looking.

When I drove into the underground parking garage, my car was taken away by a valet to be washed and detailed in the basement while I was being transformed into a goddess.

"Um, I have an appointment with The Messiah," I said, somehow managing to keep a straight face.

He was taking a short break, I was told, and would be back shortly. Meanwhile, I was treated like royalty. The receptionist brought me a cup of exotic tea and a choice of magazines.

Hardly had I been seated in a chair when a tiny, smiling Asian woman came and started fussing with my hands, clucking over my short nails.

"Oh, why you don't have long nails?" she asked, looking shocked.

"I can't. I'm a pianist," I told her.

"Oh, too bad. A shame, cluck, cluck. Such beautiful hands should have long, beautiful nails to show them off! Don't you want some nice, long acrylic nails?"

"No! Didn't you hear me? I'm a pianist! I can't play with long nails," I explained. "They catch between the keys and tear off, even at this length."

She was clearly very disappointed but started filing away at my stubs anyway.

A gorgeous, effeminate young man flitted by, did a double take and skidded to a stop.

"Oh my god," he stage whispered. "Is that your real hair?"

"Um, yes," I said.

"But it's so long and thick and blonde! Are those extensions?"

"What are extensions?" I asked. He looked at me like I was from another planet.

"Oh. Is it dyed?"

"No," I said, getting a little offended.

Where I come from, you look how you look, and nobody cares. God blesses you anyway, okay?

He hesitated, then asked, "Are you wearing contact lenses?"

"Why?"

"Your eyes are just so, so, so…blue!"

"And what big teeth I have, right?" I joked.

"Huh?"

"Never mind. You're eyes are blue, too," I commented.

"*I'm* wearing contacts," he said. "Everybody wants blue eyes these days. They're very fashionable."

This was way weird, even more so when he grabbed one of my breasts and squeezed it reverently. "And your breasts are real, too," he breathed, dumbfounded.

"Yes! Yes! Everything is real! Get your hands off me! Why are you asking me these questions?"

"Don't take that bitchy tone with me, honey! I'm just trying to say that everybody in this town wishes they looked like you! You are a stylist's dream. Look what *I* have to work with."

He pointed across the room to a pretty young brunette with gorgeous big brown eyes and a perfectly toned body.

"I don't see anything wrong with her," I said.

He sighed, martyr to his fate and my stupidity. I could tell he was looking for something to criticize, and he found it.

"Your *hands!* Oh my lord. How come your nails are so short?"

"Because I'm a pianist," I growled.

"Oh, you poor thing," he said, "Well, everybody has some flaw."
He whisked away to tart up the poor, hopeless brunette.

The Messiah was a dark, little wiry bow-legged guy with wild, oily-looking black hair. I assumed he was Italian until he told me his parents had come from Mexico.

"So, what's your real name?" I asked, amused.

He didn't want to tell me, but I can be pretty persuasive when I want to be.

"Okay, I'll tell you, but don't tell anyone," he confided, "My real name is Carlos. But don't ever call me that. I am The Messiah!"

The first thing he did was sit me down in a chair and stare at me from every angle.

Then he got up close to me and examined every detail of my face.

"Do you know God," he whispered, inches from my nose.

"Well, yeah."

"Do you believe in reincarnation?" he whispered.

"Yes, actually, I do," I said.

"Good, because I remember you," he said.

"You do?"

"Yes." He breathed. "You were Mary Magdalene."

Whatever!

By the time the Messiah finished with me seven hours had gone by, everyone else had gone home, and I was convinced he was a borderline psychotic. But when I saw the end result of those hours in the chair I didn't care who he thought I was or that my whole body ached from sitting still for so long. He had literally given me a halo! My long golden hair was full of swirling lights that started at the crown and spiraled down to the ends. I saw why everyone put up with his Messiah delusion, the guy was a genius. I couldn't stop playing with my hair, staring at my reflection in every available surface. Then he started on my face. By the time I left the salon I was super gorgeous, even with my stubby nails.

The Messiah, so thrilled was he to have Mary Magdalene back in his life, insisted on being my personal stylist, and he had a fashion designer friend, (formerly the Apostle Thomas) who agreed to dress me as long as I mentioned him whenever I appeared in public.

I was ready to perform for Sparky Goldstein.

The night of the show, the music room at Genghis Cohen was packed. I thought this was due to Reuben's superior management skills, or word spread by the Messiah through the salon, but from the snatches of conversation I heard from the audience, apparently everyone in L.A. wanted to see how Cupcake's latest victim was holding up.

So, my band and I did a bunch of my songs and danced around tossing our fabulous hair and so on and someone videotaped the show.

For a while I couldn't see Reuben anywhere, but when I got off the stage he was standing there next to an angry-looking old guy with an oxygen tank.

"What's doin?" growled the old man.

"Evie, Sparky, Sparky, Evie. Isn't she gorgeous? Whaddya think?" said Reuben.

"Yeah, yeah," said Sparky, wheezing into his oxygen mask. "Come over to my house tomorra. We'll figure out what to do with ya."

"What did you think of my music?" I asked Sparky.

"Aaaargh. I hate music. I watch football."

"*Excuse me?*"

I guess he realized he'd stuck his foot in it, what with me being a musician plus a woman, which made it very likely I didn't give a fig about football, because he quickly changed his tune.

"I loved it! I absolutely loved it! You're gonna be huge!" he roared, patting me on the shoulder. "Reuben, take me home. I'm too old for this crap."

"So, should we have her do a showcase for your buddies at the label?" asked Reuben.

"Showcase, schmocase. Forget about it. You got your deal, kid. Don't worry about a thing."

Whoopee!

PLASTIC SURGERY

"Listen, Princess, how would you like to get rid of those chicken pox scars on your face?" asked The Messiah. He darted about in front of me, playing with my hair.

I was instantly worried. My stylist was an expert at putting me down, so I would continue to believe I needed his advice.

"What chicken pox scars?" I asked.

He whipped out his loup and turned me towards the window. (For those of you who don't know, a loup is a magnifying device for looking at the tiny pictures on a photographer's contact sheet. It looks a lot like a shot glass, and since I can't get the same answer twice as to its spelling, I'll spell it however I want, thank you).

The Messiah grabbed my face and started examining my skin up close, through this magnifying device. I felt like I was in a Terry Gilliam movie, with a bunch of scientists giving me the fish eye before they sent me back in time to the wrong year.

"There, and there, and here's another one," he said.

I scowled and shook his hands away.

"Stop it, Carlos," I said. He hated it when I used his real name. He said it made him feel like a servant. I was like, *Of course you're a servant, duh! I pay you!*

"Arrrgh! Not Carlos!" he said dramatically. "Don't scowl." He stuck his thumb between my eyebrows and rubbed so hard I checked in the mirror for a dent. "You're old enough to get wrinkles."

I decided not to respond to this catty remark.

"Of course you're going to see flaws in my skin if you look at it *that* closely," I said irritably. "You'll find flaws in *everyone's* skin if you look at it *that* closely."

He pulled a vial of cocaine from his trouser pocket and took a big sniff out of the cap.

"Okay! If you want to walk around with a bunch of scars on your face that's fine with me," he said, disdainful of what he called my granola-and-Jesus-sandals approach to beauty.

"It's just that there's an opportunity for you to get a six thousand dollar laser procedure done for free. I mean, you're beautiful and everything, but there's nothing wrong with being *perfect*."

"What is this obsession with being *perfect?*" I asked. "If a couple of practically invisible scars on my face don't bother me, why should they bother anyone else? I'm a musician, not a fashion model."

"But you're going to be on *television,* Evie," he said, scandalized. "It's one thing to be on stage wearing makeup, but when you're on *television* every little defect shows up! Everyone knows that!" He sniffed loudly. "Why should I spend all this time and energy making your hair perfect when you're going around with scars on your face?"

"Oh, I see, my two or three minuscule chicken pox scars are making your artwork look bad."

"Yes! I'm glad you get it!" The Messiah snorted some more coke and I saw a tiny blood vessel burst in his left eye. Suddenly I realized what he had said.

"What do you mean, I'm going to be on television? My manager hasn't said anything about it."

"This isn't through your manager, it's through me," The Messiah said. "You should let me be your manager."

"You also think you should be my producer, but you don't know a thing about making records. Stick to hair," I said.

"I'm just trying to help you, Evie. Anyway, if you get this laser procedure done your band will be on television."

"Your *hairstyles* will be on television, you mean. Would you kindly explain what you are talking about?"

It seemed that one of his clients, an actress, was going to host a segment for "E" Entertainment Channel on this new *virtually painless* laser skin resurfacing technique. (For those of you living under the bridge, "E!" is a big major important entertainment show everybody watches in Los Angeles). They were looking for a volunteer to be on the program.

"Who do I know who could use some publicity? Naturally, I thought of you."

The Messiah blew his nose and continued, "You'll be interviewed and then filmed performing. It could lead to a record deal faster than anything Reuben and Sparky are doing for you."

Well! This sounded very tempting. I really didn't give a rat's patooty about my chicken pox scars, but what completely self-obsessed performer is going to turn down an opportunity to be on television? Hello!

I agreed to at least meet with the actress who was hosting the show.

Bebby Rae was a svelte, gorgeous blonde from Texas who made a point of telling me up front that she had slept with Warren Beatty. Even though I had the impression that just about everyone except me and maybe Jodie Foster had slept with Warren Beatty, I couldn't help being a little in awe of her access to the inner circle of Hollywood.

She seemed like she was trying hard to convince me that she was a really nice person, very down to earth, a grits and horses kind of girl. On closer inspection, however, Bebby Rae's breasts were a little too round to be natural and her upper face never moved when she spoke. She reminded me of that alien dressed up like a girl in *Mars Attacks*. I imagined Bebby Rae suddenly going mad and trying to bite a hole in my face.

"What's so funny?" asked Bebby Rae.

"Oh, I was just thinking about a movie I saw. Never mind."

I was still new to this whole body enhancement thing—something I never felt I needed, being genetically predisposed to look like Barbie as I am.

When I told Bebby Rae this, she said a couple of snippy things I felt bordered on latent hostility, but since she kept flashing her perfect smile with nary a frown line in sight, I couldn't be sure. I wondered if I should say something reassuring like, "Oh, Bebby, I really hate myself just as much as you do, I just express it differently."

Forget it.

"So how is this thing done?" I asked.

Bebby Rae opened her briefcase, pulled out some glossy brochures, and got down to business.

The first part of the segment would be shot in the Beverly Hills offices of the famous Dr. Phlake, Plastic Surgeon to the Stars.

"I've never heard of him," I said.

"He's the best," she said authoritatively. "You'll be in excellent hands."

"Oh, so you know him," I said.

She giggled. "Actually, I've never heard of him either," she admitted.

"So does Warren Beatty have a big you know what?"

"Excuse me?"

"Nothing."

"So, Dr. Phlake has performed this *virtually painless* procedure exactly 3,524 times," Bebby informed me. "He has never had a problem with a patient."

"It only takes once," I said. "Has he ever done it on TV?"

"Dr. Phlake is an *artiste*. He is accustomed to performing in front of an audience."

This got her all excited.

"Think of it this way!" She made an imaginary frame with her hands. "The first part of the show will be him creating a work of art (you!) before the eyes of the world. The second part will be you sharing your art, your wonderful music, with the world."

"Have you heard my music?" I asked.

"Well, no, but I've heard a lot about it. Just think! Two artists sharing the spotlight," she gushed.

"Yeah, I get it, Bebby."

"Okay. So we give you a couple of Valium," she began.

"Hold it. I thought you said this was no big deal."

"Just a little Valium," she said innocently. "I mean, the procedure is *virtually painless*, but the doctor wants you nice and relaxed. Then we'll ask you why you're getting it done. Let's go over it." She held up an imaginary microphone. "Why have you decided to have this procedure done, Miss Evie?"

"Because our mutual hairdresser, The Messiah of Beverly Hills, thinks my chicken pox scars are undermining the wonderfulness of his expensive work on my coiffure," I said.

"Now," admonished Bebby Rae in her soft Texan drawl, "don't be so hard on him! He's just looking out for your welfare as one of the Beautiful People. I was a little pissed off when my own plastic surgeon asked me didn't I think those pesky floating ribs were spoiling the line of my dresses, but you know what, he was right!"

Bebby Rae stood up and modeled her artificially gorgeous torso. "Now I can wear absolutely anything."

"Ouch!" I said. "Didn't that hurt?"

"Well, you know," she said, avoiding my eyes. "It's not that bad. After all, I have to be perfect! I'm on television!"

I wondered if there was a twelve-step program for surgery addicts if I accidentally became one. After all, I did have a band to promote.

"So then what happens?" I asked.

"After your initial interview you'll be prepped with some local anesthetic, which is injected into your face—"

"Injected into my *face*? I'm already on Valium and now I'm getting needles in my face? I thought you said this was painless!" I said apprehensively.

"It is! It is! *Virtually!* It feels exactly like a hot rubber band being snapped lightly against your skin." She illustrated by taking my hand and flicking her beautifully manicured fingernail against the inside of my wrist, using what I felt was excessive force.

"Ow!" I said, watching a red welt form on my tender skin.

She ignored me.

"Then," she continued, "Dr. Phlake will put protective caps over your eyes, and go over your face lightly with the laser beam. This new laser just takes off the surface layers of the skin, it doesn't go as deep as the regular laser treatment, so it's not technically considered invasive or even surgery."

"Okay," I said slowly. "I still don't get why I'm getting needles stuck in my face if it's not that bad."

"Again, honey, it's because you'll be on camera and they don't want you to move or talk while the procedure is being done, so the doctor can explain it as he works."

"Oh."

"After that you'll be bandaged up for about three days, and if you're careful to stay out of the sun, in two weeks you should be ready for your close up!"

"Yeah, now tell me about that part," I said.

She explained that when I was healed the television crew would come and tape my next concert in Hollywood and interview me again and I would be more beautiful and famous than ever.

"A couple of minutes of discomfort with a huge payoff in major television exposure," said Bebby Rae.

That sounded good to me. Besides, if Bebby Rae could handle someone sawing her ribs off and stuffing her chest with silicone, how bad could being flicked with a hot rubber band be?

"I'll do it," I said.

She handed me a stack of papers to sign.

The morning of the procedure, The Messiah picked me up and drove me to Beverly Hills. When we arrived at the plastic surgeon's office, the television crew was rushing around setting up equipment. A skinny girl with a headset and a clipboard hustled me into an examining room, where my face was scrubbed by an assistant and my hairline wrapped in a thick layer of surgical gauze. Then I waited around until Bebby Rae appeared, looking very chic and businesslike in her tailored-for-TV suit and freshly collagened lips. She raced over to me waving a cordless microphone and before I knew it I was freezing to death in the interview chair, wearing a surgical gown, reeling from the two Valiums she had made me swallow.

I noticed The Messiah staring at me from the shadows with an expression that could have been either concern or cruel anticipation.

I thought, *Oh my God, he's the Angel of Death. He has brought me to my demise.*

Nah.

I was then introduced to Dr. Phlake, a white-haired guy with amazingly bushy eyebrows.

It may be a lame association due to having seen too many pictures of Einstein, but in my mind bushy eyebrows are a sign of competence. I was instantly reassured and smiled while he took some "before" Polaroids.

"Lights!" someone yelled. "Okay, everybody quiet!"

Bebby Rae posed in front of the camera with a practiced smile of winning enthusiasm. "Ready, Scotty," she chirped.

"Okay, roll it!" said Scotty.

Bebby Rae surprised me by snapping instantly into talk-show host mode. I mean, I knew she was an actress, but since she'd lied about knowing my plastic surgeon and possibly Warren Beatty, I had decided she was completely insane and a pathological liar, to boot. But then I've heard that all the really successful actors are pathological liars. Either that or they are sleeping with the right people. Bebby Rae was working. Maybe she was telling the truth about Warren Beatty, after all.

My reverie was broken by Bebby Rae saying something flattering and exaggerated like, "So, Miss Evie, you're a popular singer around our *fabulous* town of Los Angeles, and as we all can see *quite a beauty* already. So what inspired you to ask renowned Beverly Hills plastic surgeon Dr. Phlake to perform this *miraculous, virtually painless* and *safe* procedure on you today?"

Well, I'm sorry, but I was having trouble taking any of this seriously, and the Valium wasn't helping.

"You mean," I grinned, "Why am I willing to have my face burned off by a total stranger on national television? Peer pressure, Bebby, sheer peer pressure. Nyark! Nyark nyark nyark!"

"Oh, Christ, Scotty, stop the tape," Bebby snapped.

"Cut!" yelled Scotty.

I slid to the floor in hysterics.

"Honey, are you all right?" Bebby Rae feigned concern until she was blocking me from the camera with her body. "Don't screw this up for me, missy," she hissed. Then she sort of smacked me round the head and told me to pull myself together.

I did my best, but I could feel my eyes bulging with suppressed laughter as I expressed my sincere belief that embarrassing chicken pox scars were ruining my chances at real stardom.

When I was finally able to bring myself to watch the final version of the show (after about two years of therapy) I saw that they had cut that bit out of the program along with just about everything else I subsequently did and said.

I can't say that I blame them.

I had promised Bebby Rae I would try my best to lie there quietly, but *you* try to be quiet when a madman is stretching your eyelids beyond normal capacity to fit a cold metal cup over your naked eyeball.

"Bloody hell!" I said, involuntarily writhing in fear. "Is that really necessary?"

I guess no one told the crew about the eyeball thing either, because several observers gasped and said, "Oh my God!" and then I heard someone retching, which didn't help me at all.

"Stop!" I yelled.

"Cut!" said Scotty.

"It's perfectly all right, my dear," said Dr. Phlake, bending over me solicitously. At least, that's what I imagined it looked like to everyone else. In reality, he was trying to capture my thrashing head so he could cover my other eye before the camera started rolling again.

"Ahh!" I squeaked into his hand as the world went dark.

"All set," said Dr. Phlake, clapping his hands together. Then he bent over me and whispered, "Don't be such a baby!"

This was when I decided that bushy eyebrows were sometimes a sign of evil.

"Rolling!" said Scotty.

Now, you may not be aware of this, but false advertising used to be a crime. Nowadays they get away with it. They say, "Oh, Christmas is wonderful!" and then tell you how to deal with holiday stress. If Christmas is so wonderful, why do I need to spend it breathing into a paper bag? Hello!

Likewise, take this *virtually painless* laser re-surfacing technique.

Even if you were a Neanderthal with primitive nerve endings to start with, several injections of local anesthetic could not disguise the fact that this little deal-ee-o did *not* feel like being "lightly snapped with a hot rubber band," as Bebby Rae had been instructed to describe it. It was more like being beaten about the head with a white hot poker.

"Ow! Ouch!" I yelled.

"Cut!"

"Are you okay?" a woman's voice called, distressed.

"She's fine!" said evil Dr. Phlake, exasperated. "Hold still, damn it," he said to me.

"Okay, roll 'em!"

"Ouch! Ouch! Help!"

After about four hours of this they decided to just edit what they had and overdub the audio later, so that it would appear that I had lain in comfortable silence on the table.

"I think we've got enough," said Scotty.

"You can stop now, Doctor," said Bebby Rae.

"I've done this procedure 4,335 times and I've never had this much trouble with a patient," said evil Dr. Phlake. He gave me a few parting snaps with the laser.

The metal cups were pulled off my bloodshot eyeballs with a disgusting sucking noise and my head was bandaged like a mummy. I was finally quiet, but no one wanted to talk to me anymore. I stared, traumatized, out from my white mask. The whole thing was too shocking to contemplate.

I believe that is the moment I went completely mad.

Anyway, I had accepted The Messiah's offer to take me home and care for me, which was a really bad idea because I had failed to mention his name on the show. He waited until the Vicodan took effect before he lit into me.

"After all the hard work I did to pull this thing together, I can't believe you guys didn't mention me on the show!" he complained. "Neither one of you!"

"Introducing people to each other is not hard work," I slurred. "Evie, this is Bebby Rae. Bebby Rae, this is Evie. Done."

The Messiah ignored me and started pacing. "Did you see Bebby's hair today? It was a work of *art*!"

"Yeah, she looked great. Could you leave me alone, please?" I said.

"And you!" he snarled, jabbing a finger at my bandaged head. "After I got you on this show, the least you could do is mention my name!"

"The show isn't about you. It's not even about me. It's about the laser, Carlos!"

"Don't call me Carlos!" he screamed.

"Get the hell out of my bedroom!" I screamed back. "Get out! Get out!" I suddenly realized I sounded just like that demon in *The Amityville Horror* and stopped. I've heard you have to be careful not to scare yourself when you're on drugs.

"You shouldn't have screamed at me like that," my stylist told me smugly, the bastard.

"Why not?" I asked.

"Because you're bleeding," he said.

I couldn't feel anything, so I got up and looked in the mirror. Fat red flowers of blood bloomed from the white gauze and oozed slowly towards my chin.

With my bruised, bloodshot eyes the effect was quite terrifying. Well, I couldn't let this gruesome little opportunity go to waste.

"Look what you've done!" I screamed. "I'm bleeding all over the place!"

Then I fainted.

Rather, I took a page from Bebby Rae's book and pretended to faint and then watched him from under my eyelashes. Naturally, he panicked.

That'll teach you, Carlos, I thought, watching him freak out.

I got a kick out of telling people that I spent the rest of my convalescence being waited on hand and foot by The Messiah, himself.

* * *

It was a relief to exchange the head swathe-type mummy bandages for a lighter dressing, but now I had a new complaint. Nobody mentioned that I would have to spend the next two weeks smelling my own charred flesh, a sickly sweet, burning corpse smell no amount of perfume or incense could mask.

Was this normal?

I called evil Dr. Phlake.

"I really think you should prepare people for this nasty smell," I said.

"Smell? What smell? There is no smell."

"Yes, there is. Surely, I'm not the only one to mention this. It's disgusting. I can't go to a restaurant. People start puking when I get close to them."

"You're imagining things," said the evil doctor, "I have performed this procedure exactly 5,674 times and no one has ever complained about a smell. Stay out of the sun. Goodbye."

Two weeks later The Messiah and Bebby Rae accompanied me to Dr. Phlake's office for the unveiling of my new visage. Dr. Phlake removed the last piece of gauze and threw it in the trash with a dramatic flourish.

"Ta da!" he said, corny as could be. He snapped some Polaroids.

"Wow!" said Bebby Rae. "Congratulations, Dr. Phlake!"

"Totally unbelievable," said The Messiah.

"I don't look any different," I said.

"Yes, you do! You look fabulous!" they insisted.

"This is exactly what I looked like before!"

"The difference is subtle, but it is there," said evil Dr. Phlake. "This is why we take the before and after pictures." He held up my Polaroids to be gushed over by the other two phonies.

They looked exactly the same to me.

"Okay, whatever," I said. "I look great. Thanks for everything. I'm going home now."

* * *

Hopefully the second half of the show, where my band was going to perform, would make all this worth it.

Not!

Three nights later Bebby Rae and the crew from "E" were supposed to show up at the nightclub where my band was playing. We pulled out all the stops.

We borrowed clothes from our favorite designer. The Messiah gave us all fantastic hair and make-up. The club was only two blocks from my house, but we ordered a white stretch limousine and drove around the block a couple of times spraying champagne and screaming at people on the street to come to the show.

The club was packed! We totally rocked! We left the stage sweating and euphoric!

Then I looked around the room. No TV crew.

"Where the hell is Bebby Rae? Where's the TV crew?" I asked The Messiah.

"I don't know," he said.

"What do you mean, you don't know?"

"They're waiting for you outside," someone said timidly.

"Outside? You mean they've been outside all this time?" My left eye started twitching.

"They didn't have a permit to shoot inside the club."

"They needed a permit to shoot in the club? You mean from the city?" I started tearing at my cuticles.

"No, from the club."

"Well, surely they knew they needed a permit! They're the crew! Why didn't they get a permit from the club?" I threw my cuticles on the floor and stomped on them.

"Either you or your manager were supposed to do it," the club booker said.

"*ME?*" I shouted. "None of this was even my idea! Are you telling me I just went through all this for *nothing?*"

Unable to pass up an opportunity to make me look stupid, The Messiah jumped in with, "I keep telling you your manager sucks."

"YOU!" I roared. "You set this up, not my manager! This is YOUR fault! YOU knew about the permit! What the hell was the point of all this if the band's not going to be on the show? Are you crazy?"

"You didn't dedicate a song to me tonight," said The Messiah. "You didn't thank me for everything I've done for you in the last few weeks."

"I don't believe this," I moaned.

"If you don't promote me, I don't have to promote you!" he said nastily.

I decided everyone involved in this fiasco was going to die, tonight if possible.

The second I stepped out of the club someone yelled, "There she is!" and I was hit by a blinding spotlight.

Bebby Rae grabbed my arm and dug her long, pointy nails in as hard as she could.

"What the hell is the matter with you?" she said. "You were supposed to get us a permit from the club."

"Don't you blame this on me, Bebby Rae!" I blazed back. "The Messiah was supposed to get the permit from the club. Not me. If you had told me you needed a permit from the club, I would have made sure you got one. Why did you leave it up to Carlos? You know what he's like."

"No, but I know what you're like," she snapped. "And don't call him Carlos!"

"Oh my God," I said. "You're ganging up on me!"

"You're selfish and ungrateful," Bebby fumed. "All this wasted time and energy. Hardly any of the first segment is usable, and tonight I ruined my hair standing out here in the freezing wind just to do you a favor."

It was eighty-five degrees.

"Okay, Bebby. What do you want to do?" I said through teeth gritted so hard I thought they would shatter into pieces and be ground to powder. "You're here, I'm here. The crew is here. Why don't we just finish what we started?"

"Fine," she snapped. "Scotty! Roll it."

"Rolling!" said Scotty.

Bebby Rae was instantly all pizzazz, flashing teeth and shiny hair. She went into her shtick. I stood beside her in my gorgeous evening gown with blood dripping down my arm from where she'd clawed me, and gave the camera my biggest Marilyn Monroe smile.

Bebby turned to me and said, "That was just a fabulous concert! So, Evie, how do you feel about the results of the new *virtually painless* laser re-surfacing procedure?"

"Why, Bebbie Rae, just look at me!" I gnashed my teeth a little for effect. "I think I am gorgeous! Just *gorgeous!*"

Bebby Rae stomped on my foot.

"Well, folks, we need to wrap this up. But tell me, Evie, if you had the opportunity to do this easy, *virtually painless* and safe procedure again, do you think you would?"

I took a deep breath, leaned right into the camera lens, and said, "No way!"

"You bitch!" screamed Bebby Rae.

"Cut!" said Scotty.

And I never had plastic surgery again.

THE GHOST OF HEPBURN MANOR

If you live in L.A. but you're not a top celebrity raking in the super bucks, sometimes you have to do little extra things to make ends meet, which you can get away with as long as no one knows about it. This can be tricky, because the way things are set up in Hollywood, everything is a catch-22.

If you're an unsigned artist and you are not Jewish or the child of a movie star, you better have some heavyweights behind you. But the heavyweights won't get behind you unless you already have some other heavyweights behind you, because they're all afraid to make the first move. I was lucky to have the help of White Buffalo Spirit, because now I had two of the heaviest heavyweights behind me, plus the top stylist, and my own designer. But I didn't have any money.

I knew that one way to handle this was to find a benefactor. A lot of artists have done this throughout history but this was Los Angeles. If you are able to find a benefactor, you have to keep it quiet, or you'll be perceived as a slut.

If you expect to get a deal based on your talent alone, you will be shut out by all the people you refuse to sleep with. But if you sleep with the people who promise to help your career, again you are perceived as a slut. No one cares about your talent.

If you persist long enough to actually get something decent recorded and try to put it out yourself, you can't get distribution for your record without air play, but you can't get air play unless your record is in the stores.

Meanwhile, everyone is saying, "Baby, you're great! You're going to be a star!" and "You're going to win a Grammy for Best New Artist, I just know it!" and "Don't give up! I know you're going to make it!" while nobody is lifting a finger to help you make that happen.

I was perfectly capable of making a good living as a session singer, and I had done that in London, but here I was told that if I got known around town as a session singer, I could forget about being taken seriously as a recording artist, no matter how good I and my songs were.

Besides that, my producers told me, I had a trademark vocal sound that I shouldn't allow other artists to have on their records, so again, no session work for me.

I was in the weird, nonsensical position of being a diva before I was even signed, trapped in a limbo I could not escape. All I could do was keep recording demos of new songs written and recorded with different producers, and hope that crabby old Sparky Goldstein would come through with a decent contract before he kicked the bucket.

The only other option open to me was to become a temp, but hello! Why should I, unsigned but a diva anyway, backed by heavyweight Jews, spend eight or nine hours of my precious composing time in an office, typing up someone else's memos?

Forget it!

When I was between recording projects I preferred to stay at home all day goofing off, reading, and playing the piano, so it made sense to accept the job of managing my apartment building, which was kind of a landmark in the area of Los Angeles called Silver Lake, which was close to my old hideout in Echo Park, but safer.

The building manager before me was a big guy with a cocaine habit named Matt who sold me his white couch for twenty-five bucks before he ran off, rather suddenly, to San Francisco with no explanation.

A few years later I ran into Matt working in a hardware store in Palm Springs, and he acted really embarrassed to see me. At first I couldn't think why, but then it occurred to me that considering what he had set me up for by giving me his job, it would have been perfectly reasonable if I had tracked him down and shot him.

At the time, however, the timing of the job offer was nothing short of miraculous. I was worried about money.

Old Sparky Goldstein was "working on things" with a certain label, but it was taking forever to get the contract put together.

"Don't worry," Sparky kept telling me, "Everything's going great. Just stay home and keep writing songs. I'm taking care of it."

But my personal manager, Reuben, who was tired of paying my bills, had started pestering me to get a job.

"Get a *job?*" I yelled. "Are you out of your mind? What about my reputation!"

"What about your bills, Evie!"

"What, you're paying them, aren't you? What's the problem?"

"The problem is I have my own bills!" Reuben shouted. "I'm not supposed to be paying your bills! You're supposed to be paying me, and I'm paying your bills! That's the problem, missy! Get those little pedicured feet of yours into some sensible shoes and hit the pavement like the rest of us!"

Like he wasn't lounging by his pool and playing golf all day long.

I was running out of bonbons and my car insurance payment was overdue, so I was pretty relieved when Big Matt came sniffling and jittering to my door and offered me his job.

"You seem to be the most responsible person in the building," he said.

"Huh?" I said.

"And you're home most of the time, which is really good, because somebody really needs to be here *all the time.*" He laughed nervously and ground his teeth a little, which I should have taken as a warning.

I had to interview with the property manager first. That was a no-brainer because I can talk anybody into anything if I want to, which is a dangerous gift for someone who never thinks about consequences.

Of course I got the job, which meant my apartment was free, and I even got a small monthly check for vacuuming and stuff, which I decided I would do when nobody was around, wearing a disguise.

My manager was so relieved he sent me more flowers.

"Thanks for the flowers, Reuben, but would you mind if I returned them and paid for my car insurance instead?"

He sighed. "I'll pay for your car insurance. Keep the goddamn flowers," he growled.

"Oh, goody," I said. "I love you, Reuben."

"Yeah, yeah, I love you, too. You better sell a lot of records, that's all I have to say."

So there I was, I had an easy, cushy job, I didn't have to pay rent anymore, and I never had to leave the building if I didn't want to. I broke out the Champers and lay back on my new couch, sipping bubbly and admiring the flowers on my table, with no idea in my pretty little head that I had just voluntarily entered my own personal Twilight Zone.

The apartment building was four stories high and had thirty-five apartments in it, as well as numerous odd closets and storage rooms.

Until I became the manager of Hepburn Manor, I had no idea what a weird place it was. The first thing I had to do (when I recovered from my hangover) was explore the entire building, including the basement and roof.

It was obvious that whoever designed the building was a raving lunatic.

A perfectly ordinary door in a perfectly ordinary straight hallway would lead at an angle into an octagonal room with barely useful triangular closets. Another apartment had a tetrahedral bedroom and a bathroom like a vertical egg. It was like a sinister fun house, designed to drive me slowly mad.

There was a rickety old-fashioned elevator that held only one person and required two hands to use, so if you lived on the fourth floor and were bringing home groceries, you had to take them up one bag at a time, making several trips to get your stuff up there. And hope that while your groceries were waiting for you in the fourth floor hallway, no one was sneaking around up there pinching your pasta and sausages.

Since I lived on the first floor, I never had to bother with the elevator or the endless stairs until I became the manager. Then I had to bother with both a great deal more than I thought reasonable, and it was because of the problem with the keys.

The supply closet was on the fourth floor, which was where the keys were kept. I thought the keys just *went* there, but later found out that Big Mike had put them there because he had lived on the fourth floor, and got sick and tired of the game I was about to learn to play. As I said, my apartment was on the first floor. If somebody needed a key, I had to climb the stairs to the fourth floor and find the key.

If I forgot to take the key that opened the supply closet, which was the only key I was allowed to keep in my possession at all times, I had to go back down to my apartment and get it, and go back upstairs. Then I would spend an indeterminable amount of time rummaging through the keys to find the one to the door in question. I would then come back down to the first floor, walk all the way to the lobby to open the front door and make sure the person who wanted in was really a tenant and not a serial killer. If the person really was the person they said they were, I then had to walk that person to where they were going and let them in. Then I had to walk back up to the fourth floor to put the key in the supply closet, then walk all the way back down to my apartment.

The tenants were constantly losing and forgetting their keys, so I usually ended up making this journey two or three times a week. On weekends and holidays I sometimes did this five or six times a night. I realize now I could have made a lot of money charging them for this service. Oh well.

Since I am a somewhat athletic person, I didn't really mind all the exercise. But the constant interruptions were fraying my nerves, and this was compounded by the fact that there were about a gazillion keys in the supply room, dating back about 60 years, most of them unlabelled. If a key was unlabelled or not hanging on the board, it could take several hours to find the right one in the box full of keys Big Matt had hidden on a shelf when he had first shown me the closet.

After a while I developed an obsession with keys, and started carrying keys with me everywhere. My keys, their keys, the keys to the doors, the keys to the keys, and they may not be the right keys, but damn it, I had keys!

One time the property manager showed up and wanted me to let him in some room to inspect something, and I didn't have the key.

"What is wrong with you? You're supposed to have the keys to every room in this building! Didn't Big Matt leave you all the keys?"

"Yes! He left me all the keys! I have the keys to everything in the Universe! Look!" I pulled keys out of my pockets, his pockets, my ears, his ears. "I just don't have the key YOU want!"

"Okay, calm down," said the property manager, patting my shoulder warily. "We probably have one at the office. I'll make a copy and bring it to you, and you can put it in a safe place and we won't have to worry about it ever again…"

Pretty soon I moved the keys into my apartment, even though the property manager had told me not to.

"What if someone broke into your place and stole all the keys? They could just rob everybody," he said.

"Yeah, well it might be kind of nice to come home and find that someone had actually sorted the damn things out finally!"

Besides the issue of the keys, there was another constant threat to my peace of mind. The plumbing in the building had never been changed, so not a week went by without a big hole being hacked into someone's wall to repair a pipe. This meant that I had to hang around waiting for the plumber, then the plasterer, then the painter, who never answered my pages and never showed up when he said he would. Between the keys and this constant parade of maintenance people, I almost never had time for my regular occupation, which was to fantasize about my soon-to-be-brilliant career, wear pink, eat bon-bons and drink champagne.

It was very annoying!

* * *

But I did learn all sorts of useful things, like how to fix a toilet by banging it with a wrench, and how to switch the telephone wires in the basement around so those unrepentant bloodsuckers at the phone company paid for my long distance calls to Europe.

The money I saved with that piece of cleverness allowed me to buy a new printer to replace the one the house kleptomaniac stole out of my car the day I was taking it to be repaired. I had forgotten to lock the car because I was blinded with rage by the discovery that some cheap thief of a landscape gardener had stolen my beautiful Ficus trees from the lobby! The trail of dropped leaves ended at the curb, and when I returned, weeping, to my car the printer was gone too. The police are useless in these situations, unless you are in Holland, where the police can usually tell you where you can buy back your stolen property, if it really means something to you.

When Hepburn Manor was built in the 1930s, the first tenants were a bunch of crazy actors from the silent movies and early talkies, back when Silver Lake was "the country" where the Hollywood people came to hunt and fish. Kathryn Hepburn had lived there, hence the name. Then Silver Lake gradually evolved into a hoity-toity artist's colony. By the time I got there, Silver Lake was coming down from having been a hoity-toity artist's colony and slowly turning into gangland. Because of this, the rent was pretty reasonable, so the building was occupied by a very diverse mix of people from all arenas of life.

Occasionally, I encountered difficult situations where I had to referee disputes between the tenants. About a third of them were the respectable young professionals who tended to be quiet, well dressed and polite and always brought the rent directly to my door with flowers and homemade enchiladas.

Other than one old lady who'd lived there forever and a couple of relatively harmless retards, the rest of the bunch were unscrupulous bastards who were always late with the rent, broke into the cars, worshipped Satan and made pornographic films in their apartments. I always knew when that was going on because someone would complain about hearing cheesy 70's disco, loud theatrical moans and the sound of naked flesh being spanked coming from next door or down the hall.

Late one night I was called upon to persuade the albino death metal goddess in 404 that she really could listen to the shrieks and groans emanating from her stereo without placing the speakers face down on the floor, which tended to keep the lady banker in 304 awake at night.

Having seen the interior of her apartment during inspection, I had made a point of avoiding Zilla in 404, which was not that hard to do since she lived like a vampire. But I could not avoid her now, with desperately baggy-eyed 304 pleading in my doorway in her nightgown. After performing a few mind-calming breathing exercises, I went and boldly knocked on Zilla's door. The hellish noise emanating from her apartment was deafening even in the hall, so I was really surprised when she heard me and answered the door.

"Hi," Zilla yelled, smiling and friendly as could be. "Come on in!" She disappeared into the bedroom to turn off the noise.

I pretended to admire her photo gallery of corpses, and made some appreciative noises over the satanic altar in her living room, on which lay a bloody dismembered chicken that was just begging to be baked at 350 with some rosemary and slivered potatoes!

She came back into the room.

"What did you think of that?" Zilla asked, looking like a death's head with her white face and pale eyes. "It's my new album."

"Well, I didn't hear very much of it," I said, one professional to another, "but it sounded like a thousand cats being skinned alive while a herd of terrified elephants thundered away from an exploding volcano."

"Yes! That's exactly what it is!"

"Well, it definitely comes across. Good job," I said. "I'm always thrilled when my recordings come out the way I hear them in my head, too."

After a bit more of this chitchat, I felt comfortable enough to bring up the reason for my visit. I explained that as a musician myself I appreciated her devotion to her craft, but could she not dredge up any sympathy for the poor pencil-pusher downstairs who, lacking our superior talent, had to get up at the crack of dawn to go to that nasty old day job?

Our little meeting was quite successful. The banker and the devil worshipper got along nicely after that, and I was pleased to have made some interesting new friends, so of course I wisely refrained from asking if anyone had seen my cat.

One peaceful plumber-free afternoon when I was relaxing with the literary equivalent of a soap opera, the handsome young actor in 201 came to my door and told me there was a terrible smell in the hallway near the lobby.

"What does it smell like?" I said.

"It smells terrible! You've got to come now!" said Gene.

How annoying! I put my champagne in the fridge and very reluctantly followed Gene down the hall.

To say the smell was terrible was a gross understatement. There was a major cloud of noxious evil death, right outside apartment 102! We both started gagging. I hastily stepped away lest I barf up my precious champagne all over the carpet (which I, of course, would have to clean).

"Did you knock?" I choked.

"No way, man! That's your job! I think the guy's dead in there!"

The possibly dead guy was another working musician who often toured, and I didn't pay much attention to his schedule since he paid his rent on time. But I realized now that I hadn't seen him in a while, maybe a couple of weeks.

Oh, great.

"I'll get the key. Will you come in with me to check on him, Gene?"

"No fuckin' way, dude! I'm not getting near no dead guy!"

He took off through the lobby out the front door.

* * *

I got the key to 102, and, after thinking about it a bit, knocked on Old Betty's door. I reckoned that after eighty some years of life, a pesky little rotted corpse probably wouldn't faze Old Betty. She finally heard me knocking and opened her door, squinting up at me through her bifocals.

"Betty," I shouted, "I think there's a dead guy in apartment 102 and I'm afraid to go in there alone. What should I do?"

"Oh, well, I suppose I'll come look with you. But it's probably just Sadie playing her tricks again. Let me get my sweater."

"Who's Sadie?" I yelled.

"You don't have to scream at me, young lady," said Betty. "Sadie used to be the manager here oh about fifty years ago. She used to patrol the halls with a gun to make sure there wasn't any hanky panky. Ever since she died stuff like this has been happening. You ever seen your TV go on and off by itself?"

"Yes, but I thought it was old wiring or something."

"No, that would be Sadie. She always was a bit of a prankster. You ever come home and find all your windows open?"

"Yes," I said slowly.

I thought I had done that.

"That would be Sadie, too. She likes to pick on the managers. Plus, you're the first girl we've had since she died. Sadie's probably jealous. She sure loved this place. She was a good manager." She smiled at the memory of gun-toting Sadie.

"Did she die in apartment 102?"

"No, she died in yours."

"What!"

"Oh, now don't you worry. She don't mean any harm. She just likes to play tricks is all, like I say. Probably she thinks you're not *busy enough.*"

She looked at me sharply when she said that.

I raised an eyebrow at her but didn't respond. One thing I've learned in this life is, never argue with an old lady. They might lose their glasses and forget the names of their own children, but they never forget the person who dared to argue with them. I knew if I so much as dared, I could say goodbye to warm cookies and badly knit secondhand sweaters, not to mention my job.

Betty crept arthritically down the hallway at my side, and told me about Sadie, who could sometimes be seen at night, a shadowy, transparent figure patrolling the halls with her gun.

"And now and then there's a nasty smell. Yep, that's the smell!" said Betty as we reached the miasma of death in front of apartment 102.

I nervously opened the door.

Old Betty stood guard while I looked in all the rooms, then in the closets, then under the bed. I even looked in the guy's instrument cases and pulled the covers off the bed in case he was melted in there somehow.

I've read about those spontaneous combustion deals where a person just bursts into flame out of the blue and all that's left is a blackened smudge and a shoe and a couple of teeth or something.

There was nothing weird in the bed.

The trash had been emptied, and the cat's food was pretty fresh, so the guy couldn't have been gone long.

I found the cat hiding under a chair.

"Here, kitty, kitty," I said, reaching under the chair persuasively.

The bastard attacked me. I yelled and yanked my arm out of reach.

"Wow! Look at that!" said Old Betty. "Scared to death, poor thing. Well, they say an animal can perceive a ghost better than a human."

"Well, can't the stupid thing tell I'm not a ghost?" I said, sucking my bleeding fingers until I remembered sucking a cat bite is a great way to get a bad case of worms.

Rule number one in parasite prevention, people: never let an animal salivate on you!

"Let's just move out real slow," said Old Betty.

We backed carefully out of the apartment, so as not to provoke the cat. When I had re-locked the door, we stood there in the hall a moment and I suddenly realized the smell was gone.

"Okay, Sadie," I yelled. "You can knock that off right now!"

Old Betty laughed. "You want a cookie?" she said. I shook my head. "How about a sweater?"

I said no thank you and grumbled back to my soap opera book and champagne, which was probably flat by now. It was.

Thanks a lot, Sadie!

CROSSDRESSING SCIENTOLOGISTS

Reuben and Sparky forbade me to date because they were planning to set me up in compromising situations with famous young actors.

"As soon as your deal gets in the papers, we get you in the tabloids," Reuben told me. "It's great publicity. Then we sue the tabloids, split the money, and voila! Everybody buys your record because they think you're a slut. Don't worry, piece of cake, you don't have to really sleep with anybody. People do it all the time."

That was fine with me, but while I was waiting to be hooked up with the hot babes, in the meantime hey, I was a young woman with hormones like everybody else. So I snuck around behind their backs and took a lover now and then.

You would have done the same!

So one night I met this gorgeous guy who was a guitarist when he wasn't coaching football. We fell in lust, but it turned out he was a cross-dresser.

He told me right up front in case I had a problem with it.

I said, "How should I know if I have a problem with it? I've never known any cross-dressers."

Once time I came home and found two of my male friends trying on my bikinis, but that didn't bother me. I thought it was hilarious.

Of course, I wasn't sleeping with them. Maybe it would have bothered me then.

This guy I liked enough to sleep with, cross-dresser or not, so I decided to give it a shot. Besides, I didn't really understand what he was talking about when he said he liked to wear women's clothes. I thought he meant he liked to wear dresses. I was wrong. It was a lot more complicated than that.

The cross-dresser was a professional athlete, a very masculine-looking guy. He had a beautiful lean, muscular body. He also had very manly teeth, big, square, white, the kind of teeth they have in Chile.

Oops, I just said where he's from.

The point is he was a very manly guy. *No way could he pull off the transvestite thing*, I thought. Come on! He had all these big white teeth, muscles all over the place and a little pencil-thin moustache that ran around his upper lip that reminded me of my favorite Jimmy Buffet song.

I think I could have handled it if he just, you know, put on a dress and that was it. After all, in many cultures it's normal for a man to wear a dress.

But he was into wearing corsets and stockings, curling his hair. He wore more makeup than I do, and had those long acrylic nails on one hand. I thought only supermarket checkers and hip-hop women were into those nails. Apparently, so are cross-dressers.

When he was a man someone would inevitably comment on them.

"Why do you have those long nails on your right hand?"

"I'm a guitarist," he'd say.

"Okay, but why are they frosty pink?"

When he was a man, he was this sexy macho beast women adored and other men regarded with jealousy.

As a girl, he'd turn into a completely different person.

I've never seen a real girl act that girly. "Do you think of this shade of lipstick works with my skin tone?" he'd lisp. "Do you like my barrette? Do you think this blouse looks good on me?"

"No! But it looks great on me!"

I'm a pretty feminine woman, so it was kind of strange to have a boyfriend who made me feel butch. I couldn't even have lesbian fantasies about him, because he was not the kind of girl I would want to sleep with. The first time we made love he wore stockings and a garter belt with frilly panties. I couldn't figure out how to get them off. It was kind of embarrassing. After all, I'm a woman, so aren't I supposed to know about things like that? I don't. Life is complicated enough without having to fiddle with a garter belt. Layers! I don't even wear underwear most of the time.

Speaking of layers, it really started to get on my nerves that we couldn't just jump into bed for five minutes like normal people. Forget about quickies in a broom closet or behind the bushes at a party. He always had about a thousand layers to take off. Even regular women don't wear that many clothes. We'd get all hot for each other and run to the bedroom, but by the time he was finally undressed I'd be asleep.

Our sex life suffered.

This was another problem: the amount of time he spent changing his clothes. He had to be a guy to go outside, but he wanted to be a girl at home. He'd get up in the morning and dress like a girl. Then he'd have to go out, so he'd change into his guy clothes. Then he'd come home and change back to a girl. Then we'd have to go somewhere and he'd change into a guy.

I'd be like, "Why don't you just wear the same thing all day like everybody else? This is crazy! You're so busy changing your clothes we don't have time for a life!"

Then he started criticizing my taste.

"I don't like your clothes," he said. *Well I don't like yours either! Hello!*

He'd try to loan me his dresses and I'd be like, "No way! I would look like a slut in that thing!" Which of course totally offended him.

Clearly I had a problem with the cross-dressing.

I said, "How come you're a cross-dresser?"

He told me that when he was a child he figured out by observing his family that at certain times in one's life it is better to be a man, and at other times it is better to be a beautiful woman.

It was fine to be a boy as a teenager, for example, especially when you were a good-looking boy like he was. But beautiful women in their twenties and thirties had a much better deal than men and ugly women that age, who were expected to work hard and raise families.

Then in your forties or so it was better to be a man again, so you could retire and have a beautiful young mistress.

So as a teenager he became a star athlete and had his pick of a million hot Latina groupies.

Then when he hit his mid-thirties he quit professional sports and spent several years as a woman, during which time he was the plaything of a wealthy older woman who must have been a total pervert, if you want my opinion.

Then he hit the age when, according to his bizarre theory, it is better to be a man again. But by now, having lost his wealthy patroness, he was too broke to have beautiful mistresses in their twenties, so he ended up with me.

Then he found out that his years as a woman had kind of screwed up his career options. You can't put that on a resume.

"What were you doing from 1996 to 2004?"

"Oh, I was a concubine."

So he ended up managing an apartment building in Hollywood, playing guitar and coaching part-time. I was okay with that. I was even okay with hating the cross-dressing, that's how much I liked him. I was willing to keep my mouth shut about it. But he knew I wanted him to just be a man and it made him uncomfortable, and finally he got so uncomfortable he became a Scientologist.

A cross-dressing athlete I could put up with, but not an athletic, cross-dressing Scientologist. Even I have my limits, okay?

THE DESIGNER SUNGLASSES

At some point around this time, I met DG, a dangerously exciting individual who came into my life, wreaked havoc and mayhem, then disappeared after stealing my dead grandmothers' rings and stiffing me for half of a $1,500.00 hairless cat.

When DG moved in with me I was about to get totally famous.

Sparky had finally come through. Lest I get caught being myself in public, thereby ruining the fake persona my manager had so painstakingly created for me, I was more or less under guard in my apartment building while negotiations for my new recording contract were taking place.

I understand that some people actually enjoy this form of imprisonment because it makes them feel special. Personally it made me feel like walking into Café Roma in Beverly Hills and yelling, "Hey, everybody! I've got bat whiskers growing out of my left buttock!"

So it was sheer boredom that got me into it. Plus I figured I wasn't disobeying my manager if I was only getting into trouble in the privacy of my own home.

The whole thing started when my well-bred but rather perverse friend Clothilde needed to dump a lover so she could start sleeping with one of my ex-boyfriends.

Clothilde owned a modeling agency and had a very complicated love life. We became good friends because we had my ex, that duplicitous scoundrel, in common, among other things.

Clothilde, who actually lived somewhere else, was often in Los Angeles on business, and I was happy to be included in her social life because her friends were all so original. Clothilde liked to keep her house filled with a number of odd sorts who destroyed her property and reputation during her absences. While certainly not advisable for ordinary folks, this kind of scandalous existence is tolerated, if not expected of someone as fabulous as Clothilde is.

For example, there was the boyfriend she described in the early throes of love as some sort of scientific museum person who turned out to be a black market taxidermist.

Then there was the male dancer with the tattoo-covered face who seduced the taxidermist when they were supposed to be landscaping her gardens.

In the life of Clothilde, everyone in the world was up to something! She liked it that way. If you weren't up to something she'd happily provide you with something to get up to. She did this for me all the time.

Whenever she was in Los Angeles, Clothilde and I liked to spend our afternoons together. We usually met at our favorite Mexican hideout in Echo Park, where no one would recognize us and which was conveniently located near the voodoo shop where we bought our "Come to Me Super Bucks" massage oil and our "Go Away Evil" aerosol spray.

There we would nibble guacamole and drink large quantities of tequila while catching up on business and complaining about the silly, brainless men that we are forced to deal with, sigh, because we are so smart and beautiful. As the hours went by and the tequila took over, we would get cozy with shared reminiscences of our less ladylike adventures, accompanied by a lot of giggling behind our hankies.

It was on such an afternoon Clothilde revealed that through her association with another agency up north, she had met a splendid guy called DG, who was one of the agency's partners. Suddenly it was DG this and DG that, which is quite irritating when you don't know the guy who has turned your usually articulate friend into a babbling twit.

"But where did 'Tattoo Face' go after the taxidermist tried to kill, stuff, and sell him to that Sheik guy?" I'd ask hopefully.

Or "What happened to those pigmy headhunters your secretary was harboring in your guest house last time you went home?"

Well! All she wanted to talk about was the amazing DG.

I had to admit he sounded kind of interesting, if only because he had to be the most spectacular liar Clothilde had ever produced.

DG's gorgeous surfer physique had inspired the most successful TV show in history!

DG had clawed his way naked across the frozen tundra to save the last albino caribou!

DG had escaped torture at the hands of an evil foreign government by playing Chopin on a dulcimer with his toes!

Well, it was better than nothing, after all, negotiations for my new contract were taking forever, and I was bored.

One day Clothilde interrupted my yawning festival by calling to say that DG (whose halo has inspired Renaissance painters since the dawn of time!) was selling his share in the agency and was coming to Hollywood to resume his acting career.

"Mm-hmm," I mumbled around the bon-bon I was nibbling.

There was an odd, suspiciously bright note in her voice. I waited for what was coming next.

"So, since it would obviously be improper for me to bring him to our boyfriend's home," said Clothilde, "I was wondering if you would put him up for a while at your apartment?"

I could hear her batting her eyelashes prettily through the telephone.

"I'm not supposed to have men around, Clothilde," I sang. "I'm the new 'available virgin,' remember?"

"We won't tell! How will anyone find out? Your manager lives on the other side of town! Come on, Evie, he's ever so much fun," she purred persuasively.

"You're trying to get rid of him, aren't you" I said.

"Well, of course! But he's very entertaining," she wheedled. "Didn't you say you were bored? And he's absolutely gorgeous."

Well! Not for me to ignobly refuse a sincere request by a friend. Besides, she was right. I was bored.

"When will he be here?" I asked.

"Tomorrow night! So will you take him?"

"Uh, uh, well, all right!"

"Great! I'll come over later for a drink and bring you his head shot."

"I'm going to get in so much trouble," I prophesied.

Later, when I was trying to remember how to use the dishwasher, Clothilde dropped by to show me an 8x10 black and white photo of my new distraction, who, to my delight, was a tall, handsome young blond in a sweater—but wait.

"Is this DG? What is this name on the bottom of the picture?" I asked.

"That's his real name," she replied. "Or so he says," she added.

"Why is his chin so big?"

"He has an implant."

I looked at her sideways.

"And what is this funny looking thing by his ear?" I asked.

"It's a scar," she said. "He says his face was blown off in the Gulf War and when they ran out of skin for the reconstruction they had to use a goat scrotum and he got an infection."

"Goat scrotum!" I screamed.

"Calm down! That's just what he said. It's probably a lie. I think he went to a quack plastic surgeon in Mexico to get rid of some acne scars and the doctor messed him up a little," she said soothingly. "It's really not that bad," she said.

We sighed.

"But it does kind of look like a drunk fisherman tried to make him some gills," she said.

"After an embarrassing homosexual episode," I embellished.

We giggled.

"Still, it's a pretty nice picture," I said politely.

"Yeah," she sighed. "It doesn't really do him justice. He's really much better looking than that."

"Okay, Clothilde, okay. I already said yes."

"Oh, thank you!"

The next evening I spent arranging my apartment into the kind of setting an artistic genius would live in. As I was strategically scattering orchestral scores across the piano and trying to figure out the best place to display my copy of *Critique of Pure Reason,* the telephone rang.

"Hi there, Evie," said a sexy, I'm-totally-full-of-myself voice. "This is DG. I'm just going to pick up my Mercedes and I'll be coming right over. Do you want me to bring anything?"

"Oh, you know, maybe some wine and cheese or something," I said, re-arranging flowers in a vase.

When we hung up I rushed around, creating more atmosphere and checking my makeup.

At seven o'clock there was a knock and DG was at the door, all six feet something of pure hunkdom. He put down a shopping bag and posed on the threshold, throwing ingratiating smiles of dazzling whiteness at imaginary paparazzi. He kissed my hand while gazing hypnotically into my eyes. He strode over to the couch, where he arranged himself in a sexy pose. Then he kicked off his loafers and put his gross surfer feet up on my coffee table next to the chocolates.

"Do you have a lot of stuff?" I asked, eyeing his oddly troll-like feet.

"Not really," he said. "I'll bring it up in a minute. Let's get to know each other a little first, shall we?" He stared at me with the intensity of a soap star. Despite the feet, what a killer!

When I unloaded the shopping bag I found that instead of the Veuve Cliquot I expected he had brought a bottle of cheap sangria and a lump of that kind of plastic cheddar even starving dogs ignore if they find it on the sidewalk.

Wait a minute, hadn't Clothilde told me DG was a Paris-trained gourmet chef?

Suddenly a Greek chorus started up in my head, chanting, "Goat scrotum, goat scrotum."

Oh my god! I hastened to the kitchen and bit the dishtowel so he wouldn't hear my laughter.

Later he went to the car, came back with rather a lot of luggage, and took over my bedroom.

"Wait a minute," I said. "That's my bedroom. You're sleeping in the living room, on the couch."

"No way. You must be joking."

"Way. This is my apartment, and that is my bed. You're sleeping on the couch."

"Excuse me, beautiful, but I don't do couches. We're both adults, right? We'll share the bed. Don't worry. Nothing's going to happen."

Yeah, right.

I wasn't bored anymore.

The next day he got down to business.

"Now look," he said, striding around like God in a towel. "I'm a star and you're a star, right? So we better start looking and acting like stars," he said.

"Ok," I said gamely.

"I don't care what your manager said, you've got to get out and be seen. Who does he think he is, anyway? His whole life revolves around you. He wouldn't even exist if it wasn't for you," he said.

"Uh-huh," I said.

"Talent like ours doesn't grow on trees. We've worked hard. We deserve to have some fun," he said.

"Oh, totally," I said, mooning and sighing. How come nobody else said stuff like that to me?

DG decided our cars weren't flashy enough, so we leased a convertible. His hair wasn't cool enough, so we went to a salon.

Now I wasn't a flashy enough passenger, even though my shiny blonde hair was created by God's own son and I had fashionably (and naturally) fat lips, so he dragged me into a shop in West Hollywood and bought me a beautiful, very expensive pair of designer sunglasses, to which, upon seeing my reflection, I promptly became addicted.

Now I, priding myself on my modesty and moderation and detachment from material things, would never spend more than five dollars on a pair of sunglasses. But now, for the first time in my life, I had sunglasses that didn't make my nose look like a miniature turnip! I looked impossibly cool and famous! It was very exciting, even if I knew DG had only bought them so *he* would look better in the car. The designer sunglasses became an indispensable part of my Hollywood costume. I still wear them nearly all the time, even though I can't see a thing when I have them on.

Everything has a price!

It was fascinating, if a little embarrassing, to observe DG's version of celebrity behavior. Tea boys, janitors, and assistants love me. I've gotten in trouble for talking to servants as though they were regular people. When I was leaving India after a strange little vacation there (which you can read about in another story), I gave a bottle of French perfume to my housekeeper, who was an "untouchable" of the lowest class. I thought she was literally going to die, she was so shocked that someone would actually give her a gift.

In other words, I'm nice. I've learned that it pays to treat people well. Be nice to the lady who washes your clothes, and she won't ruin your best lingerie. Be nice to the guy at the taco stand, and he won't chop cockroaches into your burrito.

Well, DG was exactly the opposite. He was the epitome of customer dissatisfaction, slamming his fists and shouting insults at hapless salespeople. I watched with a kind of mystified awe as he drove waiters practically to suicide with his impossible demands.

The more upset people got the more he yelled, laughing maniacally at their discomfort with sadistic glee. One afternoon he took me to lunch at a popular place in Sunset Plaza, where he proceeded to mesmerize the entire restaurant by alternately screaming abuse at the waiter and acting out Monty Python skits at the top of his voice.

* * *

Well, unbeknownst to him, all this yelling was shifting his chin implant around, and finally the bit of goat scrotum that held the implant in place opened up.

We were stuck in traffic, fighting in the car when it happened. We were fighting because DG freaked out when I asked him to get me some tampons while he was in the store.

I have a big problem with men who can't handle the realities of femaleness. If you don't know what a cervix is or can't say the word vagina, don't even talk to me.

"Hello," I said, "How old are you? How many girlfriends have you had that you're this squeamish about menstruation? Are you secretly gay?"

"I'm not gay," he shouted. "I just don't want anything to do with tampons or periods or any disgusting thing like that."

We had the convertible's top down, so the people in the cars around us got to hear about how it was bad enough that I liked oral sex and refused to do my own laundry, I never cooked a proper dinner for him.

DG went on and on about what a terrible girlfriend I am and now he had to deal with the hideous and disgusting processes that gave me the ability to bring life into the world.

"I'm actually kind of proud of that, asshole!" I yelled. "Where do you think you came from, you prick!"

"Hurray!" yelled the women in the other cars.

"I'm just saying I don't want to hear about it!" he yelled. "Buy your own damn tampons and don't come near me until you're done with all that!"

"Yeah!" yelled the fags in the other cars (we were in West Hollywood).

"Get the hell out of my apartment then, you moron! Go back to Iowa or wherever you're really from!"

"Ooohhhh, that was mean!" yelled the audience in the other cars.

"You bitch!" DG screamed. "How dare you say I'm from Iowa! That is the most insulting thing you've ever said to me!"

This is when I noticed the skin at the edge of his chin starting to tear.

"Oh my god! Shut up!" I said.

"What's the matter?" said DG.

"DG," I said quietly, "There's a hole in your chin."

"There is?" he said, looking in the mirror. "Wow, that's weird. I can't even feel it. Well, I guess it's nothing to worry about then, is it? Where do you want to go for dinner? Beverly Hills?"

"Maybe we should go to the doctor," I said.

"Oh, stop overreacting. Why do you always have to overreact to everything?"

"I'm not overreacting! I'm just amazed that someone as vain as you are could even think of dining in the plastic surgery capitol of the world with a huge embarrassing hole in your chin."

"Oh, come on, no one will even notice. It's not that big. Is it? Is it really obvious? 'Cause I really want to eat in Beverly Hills tonight."

The next day the hole was bigger, about the size of a dime, and something shiny was beginning to protrude from it. I knew it was the implant, not bone, but I couldn't help imagining his entire skull suddenly popping out of the hole in his chin as we drove down the freeway.

I wondered if that could be construed as a traffic violation. You can get a ticket for just about anything in Los Angeles, even if you're dead. I saw a guy get shot in the head in his car once. He was parked in a loading zone. Sure enough, five minutes later a parking enforcement officer came along and put a ticket on his windshield.

What a great postcard that would have made. "Wish you were here!"

As I stared with nauseated horror, the wound began to leak cloudy yellowish fluid down the front of his pale blue linen shirt.

Should I tell him? I panicked.

This was worse than the time I realized one of my boyfriends had a tiny spider living in his nose. How do you tell someone they have a spider in their nose?

"Look in the mirror, DG," I finally said.

"Oh my god," he said, turning white.

"You'd better let me take you to my doctor," I said.

"No, no, it's nothing, it'll be fine," he said, dabbing at his dripping chin with his sleeve and turning green.

"What do you mean, fine!" I said, "Your stupid chin implant is coming out of your face right in front of God and everybody, and you think it's fine? I'm taking you to the doctor!"

Whether the story about having his face blown off in the Gulf War or the story about the Mexican quack was true, DG was obviously terrified of doctors. He was freaking out so badly I had to drive. Then when we got to my doctor's office I had to pry him out of the car and hit his fingers until he let go of the door. He cowered, trembling like a puppy on the examining table while we waited for the doctor. I tried to comfort him, but he backed away from me into the corner. His teeth started chattering violently, which reminded me of my skull-falling-out fantasy and made me want to laugh so I had to turn away for a moment and bite my hand really hard.

"I see you took my advice," Doctor Schmidt said to me when he came in.

"What do you mean?" I said.

"Boyfriend." He pointed at DG.

Then I remembered that the last time I had seen Doctor Schmidt I had come in with chest pains, thinking I was having a heart attack. Dr. Schmidt was an old guy who had been a medic in World War II. He wasn't the most sympathetic of doctors. His bedside manner sucked, but I liked him because he was straightforward and honest, a rarity in this town full of liars. After finding nothing wrong with my heart, he stared at me speculatively for a few minutes. Then suddenly he poked me really hard in the chest. I almost collapsed from the pain.

"I know what's wrong with you," he said. "You're all stressed out. Stop working so much. Go find yourself a boyfriend."

So he was referring to the fact that I had apparently taken his advice, although having DG around was hardly reducing my stress level.

"What's the problem here?" he now said to DG.

I explained because DG was totally paralyzed with fear.

DG gibbered and moaned as Doctor Schmidt poked around his chin.

Doctor Schmidt thought this was hilarious and handed him a stuffed bunny. "Hold that," he said and then suddenly he yanked out DG's chin implant.

DG and I screamed.

DG fainted.

Doctor Schmidt laughed for about ten minutes and then handed me the stuffed bunny. "Hold that," he said, and taped up DG's chin.

"That'll be $140.00," said Doctor Schmidt. "Chin implant!" he snorted as he left the room. "Idiot."

Not long after this, my manager called.

"We're moving you to Beverly Hills. It's better for your image," Reuben told me. "Go find an apartment. I'll bring you some money."

I fell in love with an apartment on Almont Drive, because it had double front doors. I envisioned myself in a gold lame gown opening my double front doors for guests, who gasped in awe of my spacious living room, the centerpiece of which was my grand piano. The enormous antique table I had inherited would fit perfectly in the dining alcove. My white couch would be replaced by a sectional upholstered in fall colored tapestry, which would be arranged, of course, around the piano.

The little bar in the foyer would be stocked with fine wines and champagnes, and my Ficus trees would flourish abundantly on the balcony, where I would hold small but important dinner parties by candlelight.

DG, who had seriously pissed off a lot of people by now, decided it was more advantageous to bask in my spotlight than pretend he had his own, so instead of staying in my old apartment like I suggested, he moved, too.

I was kind of reluctant about it, but what could I do? I couldn't put him out on the street after we had spent all his money pretending to be superstars.

He could still charm the knickers off me if he wanted to, but he was starting to get on my nerves with his shenanigans. For example, I had specifically ordered him to let me handle the move, but then I made the mistake of leaving him behind at the old apartment with the moving men while I went to Beverly Hills have a meeting with my manager.

A couple of hours later the moving men crashed into my new apartment, dumped a load of broken glass and firewood in the middle of my living room and left, slamming the double doors behind them.

"Damn it," I shouted at DG, who was entertaining the Persian children next door by sunbathing nude on the balcony.

"Did you piss off the movers? I told you to leave those guys alone! Look what they did to my great-grandmother's table! My paintings! My lamps!"

"So what?" said DG, "Make them pay for it and get some new stuff! That stuff was all old anyway."

"They were antiques! They're supposed to be old!" I screamed.

Suddenly I realized that he had deliberately goaded them into destroying my furniture because *he didn't like my furniture*, and he thought he could make them pay for new furniture *that was more to his taste*. Wait a minute. Was this guy trying to take over my life? I began to regard him with suspicion.

Not having much choice, I called the moving company to complain about the mistreatment of my belongings and demand compensation. The owner personally came to the phone and said, through gritted teeth that if I liked being able to move around without mechanical assistance I would just forget about what happened to my stuff. Not only that, but I should consider myself lucky that he wasn't going to make my psychotic boyfriend pay for the movers' anger management sessions.

After we had replaced the furniture with more modern stuff (which I secretly liked, but I wasn't about to tell *him* that) DG decided our new life wasn't complete without a fancy oriental hairless cat. One of our celebrity photographer friends owned one, and DG was jealous.

It was a small, strange looking creature, with bat ears and blue skin, and was worth $1500. I kind of missed having a pet, so I gave DG half the money for the cat. A week later there was still no cat.

"Where's the cat?" I asked.

"Oh, these cats are very special," DG said. "They can't be taken from their mothers for at least three months because they develop all kinds of mental and emotional problems."

"That's ridiculous," I said.

"No, I'm serious. Evie, think about it. This cat is already expensive. You want to pay for an animal shrink on top of that?"

"Well, no."

"All right then, you'll just have to wait."

Around the time I realized DG was out of money, suspiciously unemployable and spookily friendless, I woke up one night and saw him standing in the near-darkness of the room, just staring at me.

"DG!" I yelled, snapping on the light.

"Scared you, didn't I," he said, with that maniacal grin of his. He had cocaine boogers in his nostrils.

"I can't take any more of this!" I yelled, "Please, God! I want to be bored again! I'll do anything!"

I became a spy. I found out that DG was giving out my phone number as his own and using my address as if I didn't live there. He was taking cash from my secret money shoe box. It began to dawn on me that his wild antics might be related to a drug habit I was unaware of. This is the behavior of serial killers, people.

Just when I was getting really worried, Clothilde called.

"Get him out of there," she said.

"What's wrong, Clothilde?"

"Just get him out of there! Get in trouble with your manager if you have to! Actually, that's a great idea! Tell your manager to come over right now!"

"But what has he done, Clothilde?" I asked.

"He swindled his partners at the agency. He stole almost a quarter of a million dollars. They are looking for him. He is not who we thought he was! He has aliases! He's wanted in twelve States! He's totally dangerous!"

Thank God, I thought.

"You have to leave," I told him.

"You can't make me," he said.

I called my manager. "There's a man in my apartment and he won't leave," I said.

As expected, my manager went ballistic. "What's a man doing in your apartment," my manager screamed. Then, also as I expected, he came up with a quick, simple solution.

"I'm bringing my gun!"

"Great!" I said. "He's bringing his gun," I told DG.

So DG disappeared after stiffing me for half of a hairless cat and stealing my dead grandmothers' rings. Now *this* is really funny! He assumes that the rings have sentimental value, so he thinks he's hurting my feelings, right? Which proves what a complete idiot he was.

Honey, this is Hollywood. Obviously I'm going to care more about the fabulous designer sunglasses he *didn't* take, right?

Screw my dead grandmothers!

BEVERLY HILLS, 90212

With DG off getting himself assassinated somewhere, things quieted down enough that I started paying more attention to what was going on around me, which seemed like an awful lot of nothing. Friends of mine who were also in the process of getting signed didn't seem to be waiting nearly as long for their contracts. Many of them were already in the studio or having CD release parties at hip places like the Viper Room on Sunset Boulevard. I was frustrated. And yes, I admit it! I was jealous.

I mentioned it to Reuben.

"Yeah," he said, "but how many of your friends are working with Huge Names like you are? This is a world class, world-wide deal you've got going on, sweetheart. You're the next Barbra, you're the next Celine. You're dealing with people at the top! You should be grateful, instead of complaining about every damn thing."

"I'm not complaining, Reuben!" I said quickly. "I'm just worried. There's something fishy about this. I have a weird feeling."

"Ah, that's just nerves, hon. Go get your hair done. You'll be working harder than you ever have in your life, so take this chance to relax. "

This didn't really make me feel better, but I tried to take Reuben's advice.

At first I was totally excited to be living in Beverly Hills, but before long I realized that unless you have a lot of money or at least a couple of friends, it wasn't a lot of fun.

My neighbors were mostly Middle Eastern families who kept to themselves. The only other American on my floor was a lonely rich woman whose husband wouldn't let her get a job, so she spent most of her time in Paris.

Reuben came by whenever he was in town, and Sparky brought me money.

Clothilde spent a couple of days with me, but she couldn't hang around indefinitely just to keep me company.

I played the piano. I had my hair done. I took walks.

On one of my leisurely little jaunts around my new neighborhood, I discovered a little deli where I bought a forty-five dollar sandwich so I could sit and watch the street for the famous people who would soon be my best friends.

While I ate, I noticed a number of women who entered the deli alone or in small groups, swathed in scarves and hidden behind big dark glasses, all headed for the semi-privacy of the back room.

At first I thought they must be a bunch of famous older actresses having a luncheon date.

How exciting! I decided to pretend I was looking for the restroom so I could see who they were and maybe get an autograph or two.

The ladies had removed their disguises and were talking quietly while they ate.

When I walked in they stopped eating and looked up at me.

I froze, staring.

These were no gracefully middle-aged Meryl Streeps and Shirley MacLaines.

Horribly disfigured, their sagging faces were barely attached to their skulls. None of them had a discernible nose, and one woman's eyelids were so distorted I doubted she could see me. Ears were displaced. Lips were swollen and contorted. Scar tissue abounded. Nevertheless, they were carefully made up in pancake and bright lipstick and huge false eyelashes, crowned with elaborate hairstyles, shocking travesties of their former selves, whatever that might have been.

I realized these poor creatures must be the victims of those early plastic surgery experiments that went horribly wrong, the ones you heard about occasionally on news shows like *60 Minutes* when the dastardly deeds of the first plastic surgeons were being exposed.

I was looking at living evidence of the tragedy behind the American beauty ideal. These women were so monstrous to behold I guessed they probably only had each other for company now. Was this what Bebby Rae and the new generation of surgery addicts would be like in a few years? I felt overwhelming pity for them.

"Can we help you?" one of them murmured, but I couldn't tell which one because nobody's mouth had moved.

Or maybe it was tears in my eyes.

"Excuse me," I managed to say. "I was just looking for the ladies' room."

"It's down the hall," one of the Halloween masks said.

"Thanks."

When word got around town that I was being championed by Sparky Goldstein himself, I started receiving calls from people who had avoided me like the plague during the Attack of the Cupcake. Now I was in a position of power! Everyone in town was just dying to work with me as soon as my contract was signed, the superficial, gutless phonies.

I was polite, friendly even. I could afford to be magnanimous, I thought, gloating in my fabulous apartment. I sipped expensive champagne and nibbled the gourmet pizza Sparky sent over twice a week.

The only producer I never heard from was the Shrimp.

Not that I cared, of course!

But out of sheer curiosity I asked Reuben to call him and tell him about my record deal.

"Forget it, Evie," Reuben told me. "He says he'd love to finish what you two started, but Cupcake still wants to kill you."

"But I didn't *do* anything!"

"I know, I know, everybody knows. Just drop it, hon, okay? There are other producers."

"Yeah, but we were doing some great stuff with those songs," I mourned.

"Well, if things change I'm sure he'll call. I gave him your phone number."

"You what?!" I screamed. "You just said Cupcake wants to kill me and you gave them my *phone* number? Are you out of your mind?"

"What's she gonna call you for? Water under the bridge. You're paranoid," said Reuben.

I knew better. Sure enough, the next morning the phone rang.

"Hello?" I said tentatively.

"YOU ATE MY CAT! MURDERER!"

I hung up on Cupcake and immediately changed my phone number, which wasn't exactly convenient since I now had about four thousand names in my address book, but at least I found out Cupcake wasn't trying to blacklist me again.

URBAN AGRICULTURE, BALCONY FARMS

The Persian children woke me up, yelling the way children do when they have found something to torture.

"Get it! There it is!"

"It's trying to escape!"

"Get out of the way, asshole! I've got a rock!"

"Wait, here's a bigger one!"

Children are natural killers, so I went downstairs in my dressing gown in case something needed to be rescued. I was expecting a wounded deer, a coyote, maybe a lost kitten.

The inexplicable object of their predatory delight was a frightened white hen who ran up and down the sidewalk, dexterously evading the ecstatic children.

A *hen* running around in the streets of Beverly Hills? I was mystified.

In Los Angeles, I knew that Mexicans and Chinese people living in the barrios kept chickens. People with ranches and farms in the Valley kept chickens.

People in Beverly Hills do not keep chickens. Do they?

Could it have fallen out of a truck delivering live birds to a fine restaurant, or the butchers? The world will never know.

"Where did you find this chicken?" I asked the children.

"She lives in the alley," a little boy said. "We play with her!"

"How long has she been in the alley?"

"Two weeks! We feed her corn! She likes to be chased!"

"Somehow I doubt that," I said. "Well, she's going to get run over sooner or later. I'll take her inside and see if I can find out where she came from."

To my amazement, the chicken was very easy to catch. She practically jumped into my arms, tucked her head with its beady little eyes into my armpit and started clucking contentedly.

The chicken followed me around the apartment while I made calls. When I sat down she hopped into my lap and settled in. She liked to be scratched gently, lifting her wings and arching her neck under my fingers. No one claimed her.

"Looks like I have a pet hen," I told Reuben when he called. "I'm calling her White Hen Spirit. She doesn't act like a chicken. She's just like a person!"

"You've got a chicken in your house? You're letting it run around in your living room? Are you crazy? Get rid of it! I mean it, Evie! Birds carry disease!"

"But Reuben, you should see her! She's very tame. I think she might have been someone's pet! She's sitting on my lap right now."

"Okay, I've always thought you were a little weird, Evie, but now…"

"All right, all right, don't have a thrombosis. I'm trying to find her a home."

"'Find it a home,' she says, like it's a poodle or something. Christ!"

"Any news from Sparky?"

"Same old shit. Tomorrow, tomorrow. I'll let ya know if anything changes."

I sighed. At least I had my chicken to keep me company.

But Reuben was right; I couldn't keep White Hen Spirit inside the apartment. She was already crapping everywhere and mangling my expensive Persian carpets with her claws.

I spread newspaper on the balcony and set out a pan of water. I bought birdseed and canned corn. I sat out there with her whenever I was home. She sat on my lap and cooed and clucked.

I had her for two weeks, and boy, did she tear up my balcony. But I didn't care. She was a really strange chicken, but she was my friend.

Using mental telepathy, smoke signals, and the telephone, I finally managed to track down Captain Bob. I figured the Indians might know what to do with a chicken-person. At least I knew they wouldn't eat her. They, more than anybody, would see that she was special.

Sure enough, one of the women from the sweat lodge had a ranch in the Valley. She rescued animals all the time. The White Hen Spirit was more than welcome.

I drove her up there and kissed her goodbye.

"Thank you for saving my life," she said.

Okay, no she didn't. But she did live out the rest of her life on the ranch, roaming free and safe, and died peacefully of old age four years later.

I don't care if you don't believe me!

After the hen left, I was lonely again, so I let the bug guy at the Beverly Hills farmer's market talk me into buying a Praying Mantis egg.

For the entomologically challenged, a Praying Mantis is a big, grotesque-looking green bug with weird giant front legs it holds together in front of it as if it is praying.

I've always had a fondness for these insects, because they are protectors of plants, they eat other more annoying bugs, and the females have the good sense to bite off the head of their mate after sex, instead of letting him hang around the house eating potato chips in his underwear while she does all the work.

The mantis egg looked like a medium-sized clump of dried mud.

"What do I do with this thing?" I asked the bug guy.

"You put it in this bag I'll give you, see, its mesh, like cheesecloth," the bug guy told me. "Hang the bag in the window for a couple of weeks. Sunlight incubates it. When it hatches you spray this liquid food on the bag. Don't let them out of the bag for at least two weeks, or they won't survive. No matter how bad you want to, *do not open the bag for at least two weeks, understand?*"

"Yes! I understand!" I said. "How many Praying Mantises are in there? Two? Four?"

"Ha! No, girlie, there's a couple more than that in there. When you do open the bag, *make sure you do it outside.*"

"Okay!"

Now, as a rule, I don't recommend taking the advice of experts, who, in my opinion, are overpaid fatheads with fancy ways of saying they don't know anything.

"What's the weather forecast for tomorrow, Bob?"

"Well, we've got this bunch of clouds here, and the wind is going that way, so I'd say there's a possibility of rain, Pete."

Why don't they just come out and say they don't know?

"Medical breakthrough! We've discovered a new drug that *might* be a cure for AIDS!"

Well, why not find out if it works before you give people false hope, shithead?

I know, I get a little carried away sometimes.

Anyway, this deal with the Praying Mantis egg turned out to be, like, the one time I wished I had taken the man's advice.

I went home and hung the mesh bag with its mud clot in my kitchen window.

"What's that thing hanging in your window?" asked Reuben when he came by with yet more flowers.

He was bringing me flowers almost every day now, with jazzy little pep cards full of encouragement. *Hang in there! Don't give up!*

"It's a Praying Mantis egg," I said.

"Sheesh, Evie! This deal better come through soon. Pet hens, Praying Mantis eggs. Why don't you get some stinkbugs and a coupla ostriches while you're at it? I got an idea, we can turn your apartment into a wildlife park, sell miniature safaris! Get some of those little kiddie cars, people can tool up and down the hallway. Instead of binoculars, we'll charge 'em ten bucks to rent a microscope so they can check out the dust mites in the pillows..."

Reuben roared with laughter, flinging himself around on the sofa, clutching his sides.

"Actually, that's a great idea," I said coldly. "That way when Sparky finally admits there's no contract at least we'll have a job."

That sobered him up, sort of.

"Look, Evie, I know you're really worried. I'm not making fun of you, honey. I know you need an outlet for that wild imagination of yours. Praying antis egg. Call me when it hatches. This I gotta see."

He kissed me and went home.

One morning I went to the kitchen to make tea and discovered the egg had hatched. I thought there might be a few, maybe five or six bugs in there. But the entire bag was black with millions, and I mean millions, of tiny, grayish green insects. Each mantis was about two millimeters long, a perfect miniature of the adult it would become.

I called Reuben.

"My Praying antis egg hatched! Oh, Reuben, you have to see them, they're absolutely adorable."

"She thinks they're adorable," Reuben said. "Well, great! Two million baby bugs to take care of ought to keep you busy for a while!"

Now I understood why the bug guy was so emphatic about keeping them in the bag until they were old enough to survive on their own. The temptation to open the bag was impossible to resist. The baby mantises were way too cute. I was dying to hold them and coo over them.

I tried really hard to leave them alone, I really did! But I just couldn't wait to see them scampering and frolicking adorably amongst the plants on my balcony. Besides, I wasn't going to try to take them *out* of the bag or anything. I just wanted to *open* the bag so I could see them better. Even if one got out, how far could it get? They were so tiny.

I opened the bag.

Now I understood why the bug guy told me to open the bag outside.

The newborn mantises were tiny, but far from helpless.

The second they realized the bag was open, which was instantly, they exploded all over the kitchen. There was no way to control them. Every surface, every wall, and the floor was covered with the tiny insects. Wailing with despair, I tiptoed among them frantically, terrified I would accidentally crush them to death. It was hopeless. They were everywhere.

When the phone rang, I snatched it off the wall, trying not to squash the crawling mantises clinging to the receiver.

"Hey, Evie!" said Reuben. "I'm coming over to see your pet bugs."

"No, Reuben! Don't come over!"

I couldn't let Reuben see this. It was way too embarrassing.

"Why the hell not?" he said, sounding exasperated. "You were all excited this morning. I thought you wanted me to come over and see them."

"I did! I do. Just not right now, I'm busy."

"You don't have a guy over there, do you? You better not be seeing anyone behind my back!"

"Of course not! How could you think such a thing! I'm, I'm *writing*, yes that's it!"

"Kee-rist. Artists!" he hung up.

A few thousand of the insects had managed to fling themselves into the living room, where they matched the carpet so closely I couldn't see them unless I got down on my hands and knees with my face inches from the floor.

They zoomed, they hopped, they leapt. But suddenly the weaker ones started to die.

Oh no! I had killed my babies! Could I put them back in the bag?

There were too many, and they were too small to just pick them up.

I ran around spraying their food on them. I scooped them onto sheets of typing paper and took them outside, sliding them carefully onto the broad green leaves of my philodendrons.

I tried catching them one by one by gently pinching their minuscule legs with tweezers. After about five hours I gave up and just opened the doors and windows wide, figuring they'd find their own way out if they were strong enough.

"Survival of the fittest," I told them, exhausted. "You're on your own."

I gave them a few days to escape before I let the maid come over to clean.

She vacuumed, polished, and washed everything, but I found Praying mantises inside my shoes, creeping across the tops of the curtains, hanging out on my headboard. Plus the ones that had made it to the plants survived, and man, they were very cool.

GANGSTAS ON
THE GREYHOUND

I believe it is very important to be open to new experiences, so if there aren't any happening I will create one for myself to keep me on my toes. Sometimes my efforts are rewarded with an encounter simply breathtaking in its weirdness.

Sparky had told me to take a vacation, so I went to Palm Springs.

Reuben was tied up in L.A., but wanted to meet with me about doing some film music, so I had to go to Los Angeles for a day or two.

After living in Los Angeles for so long I had become a transportation snob, with an attachment to my vehicle I suspected was unhealthy. So I decided to do a little experiment and take the Greyhound bus back to town instead of my car, to see exactly how deeply snobby I had become.

And you know what I found out? I actually enjoyed walking five miles from my borrowed apartment to the Greyhound station in the broiling desert sun with a heavy shoulder bag pulling my neck out of joint!

I was like, wow! This is kind of hard! When I finally limped, dizzy and sweaty, into the bus station I felt like a total hero.

People who never use public transportation have no idea what they're missing. It is fascinating to see how people behave in uncontrolled situations.

"You'd never see this in the offices of Beluga, Rogue, and

Magnum," I thought as a couple of toothless speed freaks snarled at each other over whose turn it was to use the pay phone.

A ninety year old man sitting near me told me he had hitch-hiked fifteen miles from Yucca Valley and was going to spend three days on the Greyhound to go visit his grandchildren. While I admired his grandfatherly fortitude, I couldn't help thinking why don't the damn grandkids, who have to be at least 40, come to him, the lazy, ungrateful wretches!

While we waited for the bus to show up I made a point of drinking often from the public fountain to prove that I was one of them, not one of those prissy bottled water snobs who can't handle a couple of germs.

I thought nobody but immigrants, hicks, and repeat traffic law violators traveled by Greyhound, so I was surprised to find it full of regular people. Some of them even seemed reasonably respectable, except for a group of sinister-looking Blood and Crip types who had taken over the entire back of the bus.

After experiencing a moment of paranoia when I realized I faced several hours in a closed space with my back to a bunch of scary-looking gangsters, I found an aisle seat. The driver got on, and we growled out of town into the open desert.

I thought about writing in my journal, but there isn't much to say about the desert once you've mentioned the sand, the sun, the hills, the sun, the heat, and the sun. I got out the crossword puzzle instead.

At the next stop my seatmate left and I moved considerately over to the window, leaving the aisle seat free. The gangsters rearranged themselves and got off the bus to smoke, talking quietly to each other in their incomprehensible gangster code language. They were wearing very clean, brightly colored new clothes that were way too big with huge, obvious jewelry and those funny stocking things on their heads, do-rags, I think they're called. Something to pull down over the face when they get the urge to rob somebody, I guess.

The tallest one noticed me staring, and sure enough, when he got back on the bus he went to get his bag and next thing I knew he was standing in the aisle next to me.

The others snickered like, look, Homey's gonna hassle the blonde.

I clicked open my ballpoint pen, prepared for battle.

The gangster pointed at the seat and said, "Yo," while looking at me with dead eyes. This was not a question.

"Go ahead," I said.

He sat down and sort of took over the area, which he really couldn't help because his clothes were so big and baggy. He nudged my arm off the rest and sprawled his feet all over the aisle in their giant sneakers. I pretended I was ignoring him and looked out of the window. I've always suspected that the Los Angeles Police Department secretly created gangster fashion. You couldn't possibly run away in that outfit.

I was a little on edge, so I took out my book and pretended to read while watching him out of the corner of my eye. After all, I was crammed against the window and there was no way to get out unless he moved. He put his head back and acted like he was going to sleep. Wait! I didn't want to get trapped in my seat by a sleeping gangster!

"Excuse me," I said politely. "Would you like to trade seats? That way you can lean on the window if you want to sleep and I can get up if I want to."

He opened his eyes and stared at me like he couldn't believe I was actually crazy enough to dare talk to him.

"Yo," he finally said. He got up with a kind of lazy grace and we traded places. But instead of going to sleep, he leaned over to take something out of his bag. I quickly resumed spying. It was a list of rental properties in Compton.

How thrilling! I thought. *He's one of those super dangerous Compton guys who are always in the newspapers!*

Then he put the list away and took out a little red leather case.

Here we go! I thought, and sure enough, the case contained several sharp instruments that were alarmingly dental in appearance.

All I had was my pen. If he went for me with one of those, what was I going to do, draw on him?

I tensed as he removed a particularly gnarly looking tool from the case. But instead of quietly taking my eye out like I expected, he proceeded to clean his fingernails, put the tool and the little red case away, and started watching *me* out of the corner of his eye.

"Yo, schnizzle whizzle?" he finally asked, pointing at the book.

"Silly airport novel," I said. He looked blank.

"Temporary boredom remedy. You ever had to wait for hours in an airport?" I said.

He shook his head.

"Have you never been on a plane?" I said condescendingly.

He shook his head slowly from side to side, looking exactly like a snake trying to hypnotize its prey.

"You've got to be kidding," I said. "I spend most of my life on planes."

He shook his head again and I snorted.

"Wow," I said, "You must live under a rock!"

We stared at each other like two cobras, each daring the other to look away first.

"Yo, snazzy fuckin' whazzy mumble fuckin' whizzy pizzy," he finally said.

"That's amazing," I said brightly, "I speak seventeen languages and I can't understand a word you're saying." We stared at each other some more, but then for some reason the ice broke and we both cracked up laughing.

"What's your name?" I asked him.

"I can't tell you that," he said, perfectly clearly.

"Why not?"

"Yo! Because then you be wantin' my autograph and shit, and me and homies been partyin' all week. I ain't up to the society scene today."

He did that turkey strut thing with his neck, which can't have been easy crammed into a little bus seat.

"Wow," I said, "I've never actually seen anyone do that before. Did you learn that from the gangster movies?"

"Get out! What are you, FBI? You wearing a wire?"

"No!" I said, "I'm totally serious! I saw this movie about gangsters and that's what they all do with their necks. It's like a kind of non-verbal punctuation."

"Girl, the movies got the moves from *us*," he said, getting ominous. "Are you fucking with me?"

"Why would I do that?" I said as innocently as I could. He looked at me warily.

"What's your name?" he asked.

"Well, I can't tell you that either," I said, playing his game.

"Why, you some big celebrity or something?"

"Something like that."

"Where's your limo, then, movie star?"

"I left it at home in Beverly Hills. How come you're not driving around in a Hummer, throwing hand grenades at school children?" I countered.

"Shit! You're the FBI. No way you'd be talking that shit to me otherwise," he said.

"I'm not FBI," I said.

"Then what's your name?" he demanded.

"Evie," I said.

He howled with laughter, flashing insanely white teeth and slapping his leg.

"Get the fuck *out*! Where's the fucking wire?" he made as if to start patting me down and I fended him off.

After putting on a great show of swearing me to secrecy he finally told me his name and made a big deal about being a member of Snoop Dogg's crew. Since I could hardly show him the respect he felt he deserved for being in such darkly illustrious company, I pretended I didn't know who Snoop was.

"You never heard of any of my crew?" he said incredulously. "Where you been, girl?"

"Europe, mostly," I said airily. "But I'm in the music business here, too. Have you heard of any of my associates?" I listed a few people I've worked with.

"Nope."

"You've got to be kidding," I said, copying him, "You've never heard of—? He's like, super famous!"

Now he was getting annoyed, so I decided I was pushing it with the power name-dropping contest and changed tactics.

"This is so interesting. It's like talking to someone from another planet," I said brightly.

That helped, so I decided to continue in the dumb blonde vein to keep him talking. He relaxed and started bragging and telling me scary, gruesome gangster stories, lapsing now and then into gibberish, clearly trying to freak me out.

But I kept laughing and saying things like "No way! You wouldn't do something like that," and generally letting him know I thought he was making it all up.

"So, like, if I wanted to get rid of someone I could just call you up and you'd go shoot them for me, right?"

"Say what?"

"Well, why not? You do all that other stuff."

"Are you out of your mind?" he said. "Next thing girlfriend (meaning me) be checking out the line-up goin' not him, not him, not him, it was *HIM*."

The bus pulled into a rest stop and he said he was going to get off for a minute.

"Don't you be putting no bugs in my bag, now, FBI girl," he said.

He came back with a packet of Starburst candies and immediately made as if to search his bag.

"You think I'm stupid enough to put a bug where you can find it?" I said, laughing.

He handed me a candy, and took one for himself. We unwrapped them. I hesitated.

"How do I know you didn't put some random freaky drug on these before you got back on the bus?" I asked. He sighed as if weighed down by the curse of his extreme untrustworthiness and traded candies with me. He put mine in his mouth.

"Ha! You just ate the bug," I said. He froze for a second, which made me laugh.

He really thought I might be with the FBI!

"Well, that's no problem. I'll just wait a little while, go to the can and smoke a cigarette. The bug'll come out in about half an hour," he said.

"Dang! Got me there," I said.

He put the rest of the candies in his pocket and again took out his little red leather case of tools. I reacted with mock terror.

"What is that, your torture kit?" I asked, cringing and gulping while he howled with laughter again.

"It's a *manicure* kit," he said. "Are you really this stupid? Don't tell me Miss FBI Evie of Beverly Hills ain't never got a manicure before? Here."

He took my hand and started doing my nails.

Oh my god! I thought. *I'm getting a manicure from a Compton gangster on the Greyhound Bus!*

Nobody can top this one, I thought.

We parted great friends in Los Angeles, where we said goodbye, stepping around the dead bodies of a couple of homeless people outside the Greyhound station downtown.

"I like your act, gangster man," I said.

"Yours is pretty good, too," he said, "Evie the FBI chick." We hugged and kissed and he gave me his phone number.

I called him a week or so later, but he was clearly back in the "hood," talking gibberish and turkey necking over the phone, so I never called him again. But for a drug-dealing, murdering criminal he gave a damn good manicure.

Yo!

THE ANGRY OLD MEN'S CLUB

As time dragged on I became increasingly suspicious that either Sparky was having us on, playing some diabolical game, or he was insanely living out the delusion of his last star-making hurrah, at my expense.

Every time I called Reuben about it, which was, like, fifteen times a day, he said the same thing.

"Don't worry! This is Sparky Goldstein we're dealing with here! He's a legend! He's a god! Sparky Goldstein won't let us down."

"But how come we haven't been called to any meetings? Why am I sitting around here and not in the studio? Shouldn't I be meeting with producers? Shouldn't I be out playing more shows? Don't these people at the label want to meet me?"

"Sparky says you don't need to worry about all that. If you want to play more gigs, go ahead," Reuben told me. "But I think you should just do what he told you to do, stay home and write more songs, hone your craft."

Now I know how bad this advice was, since I can write songs in my sleep and would have benefitted more, psychologically and otherwise, from being out where people could see and hear me, but being an artist and desperately insecure as we artists often are, I really wanted to believe these people knew what they were doing. It was even more important to believe that they cared about me.

I have learned that in business, especially in the music business, assuming people actually care is a big mistake. Oh, people in business care about you, sure! When they're getting your money or taking advantage of you in some way! Now whenever I see a product that has anything like "Because we care" in its advertising slogan, I avoid it like the plague.

When somebody says, "Evie, I care about you," I know right away they're out to get me.

So I wanted to believe they cared, but I was still suspicious.

"Could you just check around quietly to find out if he really is talking to all these people he says he is?" I said to Reuben. "Can't you at least find out what's going on? You're my manager; you're supposed to be protecting me!"

"You want to lose this deal? If Sparky finds out I'm checking up on him it could piss him off and blow the whole thing. Plus, ha, ha, he's paying your bills now, so that's another reason to keep quiet," he said. "I can't afford you now that you've moved to Beverly Hills, ha, ha ha!"

"That wasn't my idea!" I yelled. "I was perfectly fine where I was. They paid me! My apartment was free! All I had to do was collect the rent and vacuum the stairs! What am I going to do if this whole thing turns out to be some fantasy of Sparky's? You're a millionaire! You have a house in Palm Springs! I have nothing! I'm the one who's going to get screwed!"

"You're not going to get screwed." Reuben laughed. "Sparky's old and he's a little nuts, maybe..."

"Please just check, Reuben, I'd feel so much better if you just would do that."

"All right, all right! Stop freaking out, Evie! It's gonna be okay."

Well, I felt that Reuben's attitude was a little too nonchalant for comfort. Was he really that confident? Or did he just not understand what was at stake for me?

So I called Sparky myself.

"What's doin'?" he growled into the phone.

"I'm calling to find out what's going on, Sparky. I've been waiting for months! Does this usually take so long?"

"Yeah, whaddya expect everything to happen overnight? There's no problem, no problem at all. People are busy. There's a new president at the label. Last guy hated my guts. I guess I must have fired him at some point, ha, ha! A lot of people are being shuffled around. I decided we're going through England on this one. My buddy, Baskin, is handling it. He's the best. It's actually better for you since you came from there. I'll tell you what. Why don't you come over here and I'll let you borrow some books I'm in. I'm in every music business book there is. I just got a new one about David Geffen. You know who he is?"

"Of course," I said.

"He was seeing Laura Nyro when I signed her, did you know I signed her?"

"Yes, Sparky."

"And I'm going to get you signed, too. Come over and get some books and I'll give you a little money to help out until the contract comes."

"Which is going to be when, exactly? I need to know, Sparky. You have no idea how crazy this is making me."

"You! What about me? You think this is how I want to spend my old age? I should hear something in a couple a days. Give it a week. Get your ass over here. I'll take you to lunch."

Sparky and I walked over to Café Roma, a few blocks from where we both lived. It was slow going, what with his plastic hip and dicky heart and all. He didn't have his oxygen tank, though. I hoped this meant his health was improving. I lived in fear of him croaking before we got off the ground.

"Now, you're going to meet some of my friends," Sparky said. "Every one of them plus me, we started the music business, made it what it is today. Which isn't saying much, in my opinion. But you might learn something. Don't let these guys bother you," he added.

"Why would they bother me?"

"We call ourselves, *The Angry Old Men's Club*. We meet here for lunch every day. You ever want to eat here, just give them my name, you can eat free. Well, it's not free, I pay for it. But any time you want, you can eat here, just give them my name, tell them Sparky Goldstein sent you."

"Thanks, Sparky, that's really nice."

"Ah, stop it."

His friends were all ancient, crabby-looking guys and I could tell by the way they looked me over they thought maybe I was some dumb bimbo Sparky was playing with because I was so impressed with his resume. As if!

But an idea he did not discourage in the least, the crazy old joker. One thing I'll say for Sparky, he knew how to get people all riled up.

"Why does a beautiful young woman hang out with an ugly old half-dead fart like me?" Sparky asked loudly. "Money! Not that I have any, of course."

"Ha! Blew it all in Vegas, didn'tcha," said a crony.

"Sparky, that's *not* why I'm hanging out with you."

"Oh, then what's the reason?"

"You invited me to lunch, Sparky!"

The other old guys did their old guy heh, heh, heh thing, clicking dentures and adjusting their hearing aids.

Sparky introduced them.

"This is so and so," he said. "He did blah blah way back when your grandma was in diapers. And that's so and so. He started the first blah blah and this and that and the other thing." Et cetera, et cetera.

I didn't learn anything, but it was certainly interesting to meet the guys I'd read about in Sparky's books. Most of them never spoke except to grunt of chuckle at something Sparky said. He was the most animated of the group, given to outrageous boasting and obscene humor. Somebody mentioned a woman they all knew.

"Ah, did you get a look at her lately?" crowed Sparky, "I wouldn't fuck her with someone else's cock!"

He glared at me across the table with an evil grin, hoping he was offending at least one person. He gave up when I didn't react.

Dude, if you grew up with my mother, you'd be pretty hard to offend, too, I thought.

So, after lunch with The Angry Old Men's Club, I walked Sparky home. I thought he'd forgotten he'd said he was going to give me some money, but he whipped out a check he'd written to me, in the amount of twenty-three thousand dollars!

I almost fainted.

"Consider this an advance on your advance," he told me. "Now go away an' stop bothering me. Everything is under control."

"See? I told you!" said Reuben when I told him about the check. "He's serious! Why would a guy write you a check for that much money if he didn't mean business? We'll hop over to the bank tomorrow and deposit it together, have dinner and celebrate. You feel better now?"

"Oh, yes! Yes!" I cried.

I read the books about the music business. History, autobiographies, biographies. Sparky was telling the truth, he was mentioned in every one of them.

But wait. It seemed like nobody had anything good to say about him.

Or if they did, it was very brief. Oh, he was a legend all right! He was definitely a star maker.

But it seems he had offered a couple of people jobs, and then when they'd relocated from the other coast with wives and kids and pets, he'd forgotten all about them.

I found out he was a compulsive gambler who won and lost enormous amounts of money, whose third wife refused to marry him unless he went to Gamblers Anonymous.

He'd signed one famous singer, not because she was great, but because he owed her husband a favor. He never even heard her voice! Lucky for her, she really was good.

Now he was trying to get me signed to a label, but the people at the label hadn't heard me. Could he really pull this off if he wasn't a CEO anymore? Was he just doing this for his buddy, Reuben? Or was it his last star-making hurrah, as he had told me?

Did I care what his motivation was?

Not really.

I called him up, pretending to tease him, but really trying to gauge his reaction.

"Hey, Sparky, I've been reading these books you loaned me and you know, a lot of these people didn't like you very much."

"Don't be silly, they're just jealous. They always talk bad about the top dog. I'm a legend. People hate that I was so successful. Did you deposit that check yet?"

"No, we're going to the bank tomorrow."

"Good. Think that'll keep you going until we wrap this up? Okay, I love you, you're fantastic, now I'm hanging up. I'm going to the doctor."

"Are you okay?" I said, concerned.

"Yeah, yeah," he said. "I had five heart attacks. You know I got a pacemaker and a plastic hip. I'll show you my scars some time. I'm indestructible! Got your songs ready? Pick out your studio, gorgeous, and call me tomorrow when you get home from the bank."

Reuben picked me up early the next morning, handsome in his blue pinstriped suit, the perfect accessory to my halo hair and designer sunglasses.

We drove over to the bank in the leisurely way of people who haven't a care in the world. I was enjoying the morning sun, I had riches to come, and everything was coming up roses, as they say. We'd decided to open new accounts in my name, but with authorization for him to take out funds with my signature of approval.

We'd deposit this much in checking, that much in savings, and keep some to play with.

"An advance on your advance! Which could be as much as a million, you know. Sparky's the greatest, right? I toldja not to worry!" Reuben laughed happily and I could see the palm trees along Wilshire Boulevard mirrored in his extra shiny white teeth as we drove along. "Didn't I? Didn't I tell you not to worry? Was I right?"

"Yes, yes, you were right, okay!" I said.

"And twenty percent of it is *mine,*" he said. "Ah, the music business. I love it!"

We laughed and joked and congratulated each other as we wove through the morning traffic in the beautiful sunshine, in beautiful Beverly Hills.

"Get a new dress this afternoon and I'll take ya to Chasen's for dinner, hon," Reuben said, patting my leg. "You know, Celine Dion is married to *her* manager."

"Yes, she is," I said.

"Think you could ever consider marrying me?"

"Reuben!"

"Just an idea I had, don't get excited. I just thought, you know, we're a great team. You're a little weird, of course," he laughed some more. "Well, not a little."

"That's enough," I said.

"Okay, okay!"

The only thing I wanted now was my contract, and to be in the recording studio making my albums, and that was all gloriously before me, tangible enough almost to touch.

Inside the marble walls of the bank we sat on expensive leather couches sipping tea while we filled out forms and handed over the check to a smiling, pretty woman in an expensive suit who expressed pleasure at doing business with such handsome, fortunate people. Then she took away our forms, identification, and the check, and was gone for quite a long time.

"I should have brought my book," joked Reuben.

When the woman finally came back she was not alone. Two guards and a frowning, impeccable bank manager were with her, and we were gravely informed that not only was Sparky's check for twenty-three grand no good, but that the account it came from had been closed for, like, thirty years.

I immediately went into shock.

The last time I had really felt violated was in Thailand when, after surviving a devastating flood, some scary guys who were guarding some nebulous unmarked political boundary tried to plant drugs in my suitcase.

That situation had been potentially life-threatening, but somehow this was worse.

This was a betrayal of my heart and soul, my music.

This was personal.

I turned on my manager, claws and teeth.

"Reuben! This is your fault! Remember my fishy feeling? I told you to check out his story! Didn't you check?"

"Hey, I'm as much in the dark as you are! Don't yell at me!"

"You're in possession of what's considered a fraudulent document, which is a federal offense and a very serious crime," said the bank manager, "The proper authorities must be contacted at once."

"Are you crazy?" I screamed. My voice echoed off the marble floor and walls. Everyone in the lobby stared. "Why would I try to open a bank account in my own name with a check I *knew* was bad? Nobody's that stupid!"

"They must be filming," someone said.

"Wow, is she an actress? She's very good," someone else commented.

Reuben went berserk.

"You bunch of stupid, fucking fascists!" yelled Reuben. "Isn't it enough the poor girl's being bamboozled by a crazy, senile old man? You want to arrest someone, I'll give ya his fucking room number at the hospital where he's having his goddamn pacemaker refibrillated or whatever! Do you know who I am? I am *Reuben Solperstein. I own* this town! You try to arrest this girl and I'll sue this bank for everything it's got, you piece of shit!"

I was like, *Wow, you go, Reuben.*

I guess my brokenhearted sobs and Reuben's obvious outrage convinced them that we were telling the truth, because after about fifteen minutes of hushed, worried debate, they simply handed me the check and let Reuben take me home, where I promptly chugged two bottles of champagne and went to bed with my teddy bear and my Praying Mantises.

Sparky was very apologetic. He said he didn't realize it was the wrong check. He had millions of checks in a drawer, he just pulled one out, he blamed the housekeeper; he blamed his accountant. He brought me six thousand in cash and took me out for lobster and didn't make any obscene remarks about having to go up on tall women because he was too short to go down on them or what he wanted to do with my breasts. He gave me a pearl necklace from Tiffany and paid my bills and loaned me his fancy car to visit my mother in Palm Springs. He called me every day just to say hello, and one afternoon he even came over, sat next to my piano, and listened to my new songs.

When I was done singing he sat quietly for a minute. Then he said, "You're a complicated lady."

"What do you mean by that?" I said.

"You're smart. Very smart. I hafta admit I'm kind of surprised. I thought you'd be a bimbo, but you're not."

"No, Sparky, I'm not."

HOLLYWOOD BIMBO

One day Sparky told me to come to his apartment.

"I think you need a new manager," Sparky said.

"How come?"

"Reuben doesn't know what he's doing. All this time I'm busting my ass for your deal, a good manager should be busting his to use mine as leverage to get you a better one. What does he do? Does the man do anything?"

"Actually, I don't know."

"Does he produce movies? Isn't that what he does?"

"I don't think he's producing anymore. He's in Palm Springs a lot. I don't really know what he does down there."

"So he's not really doing anything for you, just waiting to rake in your dough, right?"

"Well..."

"Has he mentioned marriage?"

"Actually, yes. He's brought it up a few times."

"That's what I thought, the schmuck! He's waiting for you to hit big so he'll be in on the dough. What a schmuck!"

I waited.

"I'd marry you if I was forty years younger."

"That's really sweet, Sparky."

"Yeah, too bad I'm so old. You need a good manager and a rich young husband who can take care of you. We need to get rid of Reuben. I'm going to get Reuben a job."

"Where?"

"At the label. Stick him in film music over there. Piece of cake. Now, I want you to go meet this friend of mine, a great manager. He's the godfather of one of my kids. His name is Burt Polk, he manages a couple of the biggest rock bands in history. I called him already. You've got a lunch meeting tomorrow. Don't miss it."

"But Sparky, Reuben will be really upset…"

"Just go meet the guy, see if you click. Don't tell Reuben."

"Okay."

Now, I really like people and I can get along with just about anyone, but I hated Burt Polk the second I laid eyes on him. I almost turned around and walked out of Jerry's Deli, where we were meeting, but I couldn't very well tell Sparky I'd walked out on him. I forced myself to go to the table and introduce myself.

Burt had already ordered without me, even though I wasn't late.

I started a list in my head.

Rude Mr. Big Shot faux pas number one: ordered before I arrived.

"I'm Evie London," I said. He chewed on some bread, barely glancing at me.

"What am I doing here?" he said.

Rude Mr. Big Shot faux pas numbers two and three: doesn't introduce himself, talks with mouth full.

"Sparky Goldstein thought we should meet."

"Why?"

"He didn't tell you?"

"No. I don't even know who you are. Are you a hooker?"

Forget the list. Everything he said pissed me off even more.

"No, I'm not a hooker! I'm a classically trained rock musician, singer, and recording artist. I've been signed before, and sold well in Europe. I've been working with a number of top producers since I came to L.A. Sparky got me a deal. He thinks I need a new manager."

"He's lying," said Mr. Major Prick.

"What?"

"There's no deal."

"What are you talking about?"

"He's done this before. Look, everybody loves the guy, but he's completely out of his mind. You should just forget about him and get on with your life."

"But he's been working on this for months with people here and in England!"

"How do you know that? Have you seen any evidence? Any memos, any proposals?"

"No, but…"

"Look, kid, forgive me, but you're really naïve, and I can tell your manager totally sucks or you wouldn't be in this position."

I decided not to mention that Reuben had been sent by the White Buffalo Spirits.

"You're probably really upset now and hate my guts."

You got that right, buster!

"But I'm telling you the truth," he continued. "You'll find out. Don't let him string you along. You're going to get hurt. Believe me, I've seen this happen before."

I drove straight to Sparky's apartment and hammered on the door until he opened it, looking surprised. I told him what Burt Polk had said.

"He told you that, huh?" Sparky said, looking worried.

"I knew it!" I shouted, "I told Reuben I thought you were making this whole thing up! Where are the deal memos? Where are the faxes? Where is the preliminary agreement? Why hasn't anyone asked to meet me?"

"Okay, I'll be honest with you. The thing through England was working, but my friend's mother died and she was like, like, a queen, or something so he had to go back to India to be king and when he left the English company said no to your deal. I've been trying different companies. I'm still trying."

"Trying how? What exactly are you doing?"

"I'm making calls! I don't have to do things the other way because of who I am! I didn't want to tell you because I didn't want you to get upset."

"Get upset?" I yelled. "Sparky, I can handle rejection! I'm not stupid! I realize my music appeals to people with a certain amount of intelligence and sophistication, which means I might be in the wrong city and the wrong country, but what upsets me is that you've been lying to me! Lying!"

"Well, yeah! What did you expect? This is the music business!"

"Whatever. What exactly do you say to these people you're calling?"

"I say I got this great girl, a great artist, they ought to sign her up! They say, is she playing anywhere? And I say no, and they think you're not ambitious enough if you're not even performing."

"But you told me to stay home and write!"

"You don't have to do everything I say. If you're a musician you should go out and perform! I thought you liked hanging around your apartment getting presents and borrowing my car. I thought you hooked up with Reuben because you wanted to be a kept woman, 'cause he's certainly no manager. I've been hoping you'd fall in love with *me*, but I'm too old for you."

Oh my god!

"So you think I'm just another Hollywood bimbo."

"Sweetheart, you're a beautiful, smart, talented young woman. You just have rotten judgment. You're too trusting."

"I can't believe this."

"Well, don't worry. I got something going on now that's gonna be huge, I mean huge! I'm gonna be the richest man in town. Then I'll give ya the money to make all the albums you want."

Sparky put on his oxygen mask and turned up the football, angry, wheezy, demented old madman that he was.

STALKER

I called Reuben and demanded he come to my apartment immediately.

"Well, looks like we've both been keeping little secrets," Reuben said. "You've been meeting with other managers, and Sparky got me a job at the label in the film division."

"That's bullshit."

"No, it isn't! He's Sparky Goldstein, he can do whatever he wants!"

"That's ridiculous and you're an idiot! I called the record label and they never heard of you or me or Sparky either, Reuben. They've never heard of us! Sparky's insane."

"And I'm an idiot, now, after everything I've done for you? Ah, sheesh, it's not such a tragedy. Anyways, I don't care about Sparky. I have something even better."

"What?"

"Well, I was gonna tell you later, but I'll tell you now. I can't manage you anymore," Reuben said.

"I wouldn't call what you've been doing 'managing' exactly," I muttered.

He ignored me.

"But it's not because Sparky got me a job. It's because," here he literally puffed out his chest and strutted around the room, the prat, "I'm running for congress."

"You're *what*?"

"Yeah. What do you think I've been doing when I'm not with you?

Playing golf? I got a campaign manager and everything. I've been giving speeches and doing functions and everything."

I stared at him with my mouth open.

"We have a contract," I hissed.

He ignored me.

"You know, I've got a speech to give at this function tonight I could really use your help with. I don't write such good speeches. I thought, you're a great writer, maybe you could help me. And we'll find you a real manager, okay? I'm not gonna just drop you. I love you, I believe in your talent, you're totally beautiful. In fact, I want to marry you."

"You *what?*"

"You heard me! Don't look so surprised! I've been telling you this for weeks. You'd make a fabulous congressman's wife. But I don't want any kids, okay? I hate kids. By the way, I bought you a watch."

"Reuben, I just found out today that my life is a lie. It's over. I'm screwed. I'm back to square one. You're acting like it's no big deal and talking about marriage. That's a little disturbing, Reuben. Not only that, you've been running for congress and you never said anything to me about it. You're *supposed* to be my manager, and instead of doing your *job* you've been running for congress behind my back and letting me go crazy all this time! Now what am I going to do!"

"Look, I know you'll get a deal. You've been recording, right? We'll find you a manager. You might just have to get a job for a little while. Come on, everybody does it! Now will you help me with my speech, please?"

"Sure," I said tiredly. "Fax it to me. Go away please, I need to throw up and get drunk and kill myself."

"Oh, don't be so dramatic," Reuben said.

A few days later I was talking on the phone to one of the producers I was writing with. We were re-working the lyrics of a chorus when he interrupted me.

"Hey, Evie, do you think your phone might be tapped? I keep hearing weird noises on the line."

"I've noticed that, too, for a couple of months. But who would tap my phone?"

"Didn't you say your manager was running for office?"

"Yeah, but big deal. And he's not my manager anymore. Anyway, we never talk about anything important. I just help him with his stupid speeches and he tries to talk me into marrying him. Like that'll make up for the whole Sparky thing."

"Well, be careful, okay? People in politics can be dangerous. Remember what happened to Marilyn Monroe, ha, ha! So anyway, I think we should do the chorus like this…"

I came down with the flu. I was sweating with fever, delirious, when Reuben faxed me his latest speech. It was worse than usual, really just unbelievably dumb. I mean, please.

It was totally embarrassing. Was Reuben losing his mind? Was his campaign manager not paying attention?

"I am surrounded by idiots and fools," I said to my Praying Mantises.

"Yes! You are!" said the mantises.

No they didn't.

I called Reuben.

"Reuben, what is this shit? You can't get up in front of people and say these trite, clichéd things. And it's not funny! Where's the wow? They're going to think you're a joke."

I honked and coughed and drank some water.

"Are you drunk? Come on, Evie, I need your help."

"I'm sick, Reuben! I've been sick for days! I need sleep! I have a temperature of a hundred and four!"

"I'm sorry you're under the weather, hon. But you're my little speech writer, and this thing is tonight."

"Damn it! I am not your speech writer! I'm sick! And I've got bills, Reuben, bills! You could throw a little campaign money my way you know, it's your fault I'm in this position! You owe me! I'm going to lose this apartment soon. You don't even care that I might be on the street!"

"You're not going to be on the street, Evie. Relax. Everything's gonna be fine. Maybe you should talk to someone, get some therapy. Will you please help me? Please?"

I blew my nose and called Reuben's campaign manager, whom I would be pleased to refer to as the Scumbag from now on.

"Have you seen this speech Reuben is planning to give?"

"Yes," said the Scumbag.

"What do you think of it?" I asked.

"I think it's terrible, as usual," said the Scumbag. "They always are until you fix them."

"But I'm sick, Scumbag. I can't do this right now. The function is tonight! This is hardly professional."

"I'm aware of that, Evie" said the Scumbag. "But you know what, I've given up."

"Why?" I asked. "You guys have been campaigning for months! You can't just drop out now."

"We have not been campaigning for months. Reuben has not been doing the things I told him to do. He's supposed to be at our office every day making calls."

"He has been at your office every day for, like, five months."

"Is that what he told you?" said the Scumbag.

"Yes."

"Because we thought he was with you every day for the past five months."

"Why would he be with me? We don't work together anymore. I've hardly seen him."

"Do you know where he is right now?"

"Yes, I just talked to him. He's at his apartment in Beverly Hills."

"Are you sure?"

"I just called him over there!"

"Okay," said the scumbag. "I need to talk to you about Reuben, Evie."

My head was throbbing. I was too sick for this.

"I'd love to chat, but I'm really, really sick right now," I said.

"We're aware of that. But this could be important. Last time I saw Reuben he'd been drinking and he took some kind of pill. Do you know what he's on?"

"First of all, Reuben doesn't drink."

"Yes, he does, Evie, I smelled it on his breath. He reeked!"

"I find that very hard to believe. Reuben hates alcohol."

"What about the pills?"

"He's got an ulcer! It was probably a Rolaid or something."

"Hmm," said the Scumbag. "Has he been acting weird with you at all, sending flowers, telling you he loves you, things like that?"

"He always sends flowers. And of course he says he loves me. The guy wants to marry me. That's kind of normal, Scumbag."

"Are you going to marry him?"

"No! I don't know if you are aware of what I just went through with him as a manager…"

"We know all about it," said the Scumbag. "Do you think your phone is tapped?"

"Some people think so, I don't know, why?"

I heard the Scumbag talking to someone else. Then he came back on the line.

"Evie, we just found out Reuben is not at his apartment."

"He probably went for a walk," I said.

"We have reason to believe that Reuben is stalking you."

"*What?* Are you crazy?"

"I'm serious, Evie. You could be in danger. Reuben's been under a lot of stress this past year. He's unstable. He's drinking and taking pills. He's not showing up for work. He's been following you around and spying on your apartment. We believe he has tapped your phone."

"What? How? Why?"

"We spoke with the building manager, who has seen Reuben on several occasions, trying to get into your apartment when you're not home."

"You've got to be kidding."

"I'm going to have you talk to a friend of mine here. He's with Threat Management."

"What the hell is that?"

"They're kind of like the FBI, but they protect celebrities. I'm putting him on the line."

Well, come on, I didn't believe any of this, but I couldn't help being a little thrilled by the weirdness of it all. The idea of Reuben stalking me was just too ludicrous, but then again, he had been getting kind of pushy lately. And he had been more pompous and vague than usual, which I thought had to do with cranial swelling due to massive ego growth.

And he did seem to know an awful lot about my activities.

And he had shown up a bunch of times without calling first.

And…hmmm…

"Find some place to spend the night. Don't talk to him. If he calls tell him to speak with your lawyer. Come to our office tomorrow."

"I'm sick!" I wailed.

"We know, but you might be dead if you don't do what we say."

"Reuben would never hurt me," I said. "He's kind of stupid, but he's not a killer."

"You don't know that."

"Sparky, I've got the flu, Reuben is stalking me, and I need to stay at your place."

"Reuben is stalking you?"

"I know; it's completely insane. But this FBI guy said I can't be home tonight."

"I'll send a car for you," said Sparky, excited by the drama, as I knew he would be, because this was exactly his kind of Frank Sinatra, cloak and dagger gangster baloney.

The next day I called my lawyer and told him what was going on. Then I spent hours at the Threat Management office, sipping Theraflu and listening to three expressionless guys explain how much danger I was in. They were very good at their job. By the end of the afternoon I was absolutely terrified of Reuben. But after a while the novelty of being scared out of my wits wore off and I started getting the sneaking feeling that this might all be a red herring, a set up.

"I'm going home," I said.

"You can't go there!" they shouted. "It's too dangerous!"

"I mean, back to Sparky's."

"We think you should seriously consider leaving the State of California. If you could go back to England that'd be even better."

"Yes, Europe is a great idea."

"No, Morocco. He'd never find her there."

"Too obvious."

"Zimbabwe."

"That'll be seven hundred dollars, by the way."

"Get it from Scumbag! This was his idea, not mine," I said.

I went to a pay phone and called Reuben's Palm Springs number.

"Hello," said Reuben.

"Hi, Reuben, it's me," I said.

"Oh hey, Evie, how you doing? Are you feeling better? Look, I'm sorry I asked you to fix my speech yesterday when you were sick. I'll be back in town tonight and I'll bring ya some chicken soup, how's that sound?"

"That sounds great. Hey, Reuben, you have absolutely no clue what's going on, do you?"

"Congressional candidate Reuben Solperstein has been accused of stalking the singer he used to manage," the newspapers said. "Evie London was not available for comment, but music business legend Sparky Goldstein, who hid the young woman in his Beverly Hills apartment during her terrible ordeal, said, 'Reuben's always been a schmuck. Somebody take this girl off my hands and give her a record deal'."

They say everybody gets fifteen minutes of fame.

I got twenty-two.

Not the fun kind, but still.

THERAPY

So, I kind of lost it there for a while. My life made no sense and I had been betrayed by people who could not be trusted, which made me look like a total idiot.

But if I made one or two bad choices it was out of ignorance, not stupidity.

There was no one to ask! I didn't have a decent mentor!

And maybe I had misinterpreted the events after the sweat lodge. Maybe Reuben was not the guy the White Buffalo Spirits were leading me to. Maybe he would have *led* to the right manager if I hadn't jumped in and agreed to give him a shot at it.

I wasn't cautious enough.

If I had been a little more patient someone would have told me that it was stupid to let an ex-film producer manage my career. The movie people and the music people hate each others' guts. No record company CEO was going to want to deal with an ex-movie guy. Especially one who said stuff like, "I could run this company better than you! Why dontcha move over and I'll be the CEO and manage Evie on the side. You can be, oh, I don't know, a Vice President," in the very first meeting with the CEO of the record company, which totally embarrassed me to death!

And how could I know that just because a guy's a living legend doesn't necessarily mean he has any integrity? There is a difference between being well-known and being notorious, people!

This is why I am no longer impressed by a resume. I don't care what's on it. You could be the biggest hotshot in the world, but guess what? That doesn't matter to me if you're a dick. If you're not an honest professional, I don't want anything to do with you, got that? No more gangsters! If we make a deal, you keep up your end, I'll keep up my end, and I don't want any crap! I've got my eye on you!

Okay, okay.

Anyway, I was in the depths of despair. How had I let this happen? Was I truly that self-loathing? Was I afraid of success? Why, since I came to Hollywood, had everything gone horribly wrong? Was it possible that I had no idea that I was really just incredibly dumb?

I *knew* I wasn't, "sleeping with the wrong people," because I had tested that bright little theory after being told that a few times.

The guys who said I was sleeping with the wrong people were always youngish, good-looking record producers, so I didn't really mind sleeping with a couple of them just to see if they were right. Guess what? None of those guys did a damn thing for my career.

Take it from me, girls. When you run away to Hollywood because somebody says you're the next Madonna or Britney, bear this in mind. If somebody tells you you're sleeping with the wrong people, screw their brains out if you want, but otherwise don't waste your time with them.

I could have sued Reuben and Sparky. I spoke to a lawyer about it and he said I definitely had a case. I thought about it. Reuben would probably sue me right back for some kind of "unpaid loan" bullshit because he had paid my phone bill a few times and kept me in large bouquets of beautiful fresh flowers for nearly a year.

Or maybe he'd pull the cry-baby act and tell everyone how I had callously led him astray with my ample charms, convinced him I could make him a billionaire, and then ruthlessly crushed his sensitive heart. Or maybe he'd try the "loss of income" angle, claiming payment for the months he'd been pretending to slog around the city trying to help make me a star.

As for Sparky, he was clearly just a crazy old man in an appalling state of health. Everybody felt sorry for him.

When I told people about the bounced checks and the months of lies, it was amazing how many people said, "Oh, poor old Sparky! He must really miss being a player!"

I was like, "What about me?"

"Oh, you've got your whole life ahead of you, hon! You'll be all right! You might have to get a *job,* though."

I couldn't deal with any of it. It was all too heartbreaking.

So I wept and gnashed my way into therapy.

I've known a lot of people in therapy so I know how they tend to go on and on about how much they love their therapist. They would just be dead without their therapist! I always thought that was really weird, until of course I realized that in Los Angeles, just because you refer to someone as your "friend" doesn't mean you actually ever talk to them, especially about important things. I could see that my raging tantrums, inability to hold a conversation, and tendency to start sobbing for no reason were a little hard on everyone.

"You need to get on Prozac," one friend told me. "I was crazy just like you before I started taking my Prozac, but now I'm just mellow all the time."

"Yeah, and your new songs suck!" I wanted to say.

But I didn't.

"Why would I want to be a pill-popping zombie?" I said instead. "I'm an artist! I need my craziness. I deserve my craziness! I earned it! My craziness is totally healthy! I want to experience the full extent of my craziness; it is mine!"

"Okay, dude. See you around."

I didn't have anyone to talk to.

Maybe a couple of hundred million pill-popping zombies could be right.

Right?

I decided to find out.

The first therapist I went to was a guy who held this grief meeting for traumatized people at his office every Wednesday night.

I felt like a total jerk there. These people had suffered serious tragedies. One person's child had been murdered. Another had been brutally raped and left for dead. One man had woken up in the morgue of a major hospital after unnecessary surgery and probably wasn't going to get much out of the trial.

"What happened to you, dear?" they asked me on my first day, when we were getting to know each other. After hearing their totally heartbreaking stories I felt like a total ass saying I was upset because I lost a record deal. Oh! Poor little "Barbie's" dream world has gone to pieces, boo hoo!

My situation was way too shallow. In the world of psychological pain, I had broken a fingernail. No, I had discovered a split end.

Now I really hated myself. I was a miserable failure even at being a miserable failure!

I couldn't even manage to be a tragic victim of circumstances properly.

I told the psychologist that I felt the group was wrong for me.

"These people really need to be here," I told him. "I'm not that bad," I said. "I don't think," I added.

He asked me to stick it out for a few weeks, just to see if I heard anything useful. I agreed reluctantly, even though I was totally embarrassed at being such an obvious imposter.

I mean, yeah, I was nuts, and I had just lost everything, my apartment, my manager, my self-esteem. But I was just feeling sorry for myself, really. It wasn't a truly hideous crime, what happened to me. My case was all about vanity and pride and wounded egos and people acting stupid so they would look important.

It seemed like a waste to pay to sit there every week listening to the group talk about totally depressing things when my life was actually fixable. So I quit the group after about eight sessions and told my aghast therapy-zombie friends I was sick of listening to everybody whining.

"That was just the wrong kind of therapy for you, Evie," they said. "You don't need a grief group, you need to talk to someone who understands the stress of our business. You're an artist. Your problems are different. Find somebody who works with music industry people."

Therapist Number Two was working with another singer I knew, and she highly recommended him. He had an office in the heart of Beverly Hills, and only worked with entertainers. I called and booked a consultation with him.

When I told him my story, he stroked his carefully manicured white beard and said, "I want you to go home and do something. Imagine that you are holding yourself as a hurt little girl, and pretend you are hugging your teddy bear. Come back next week and let me know if it helps. That'll be a hundred and fifty dollars. Leave a check with my secretary."

I was like, dude, that's exactly the kind of crap that made me nuts!

Later I asked my singer friend about *her* session with him that day.

"Oh Dr. So-and-so is just amazing, he's a true miracle worker. I was so depressed until I saw him. Now I feel just fantastic!" she gushed.

"Why, what did he say?" I asked. I knew I was prying, but hey, she didn't have to answer the question, right?

"He said I should just visualize holding myself as a hurt little girl, and give myself a teddy bear to hug."

"You're kidding," I said. "That's exactly what he said to me."

"Isn't he just a genius?"

No! He's a total fraud! I wanted to say.

But I didn't.

Therapist Number Three was an aging surfer type whose office was near the beach in Santa Monica. He acted stoned and said "dude" a lot.

"Whoa, dude, you are seriously stressed out," he said.

"Duh!"

We couldn't take each other seriously.

Finally, I heard about a clinic located in Beverly Hills, but they took poor people, too, so I figured they might actually give a damn.

There, I met with a woman of my own age we'll call Kate. She was very bright and straightforward, and I could tell she was really interested in helping me.

I told Kate I wasn't having much luck finding a therapist I could work with. When I told her about the other guys I'd seen, she laughed. I liked her right away. We decided to give it a shot.

My first session with Kate, we started out with me telling her the story of my life.

I told her how I had driven my parents crazy and left home young and ran away to Europe and become a minor star, and how I'd come to be baptized by the last exorcist in England and then was lured to Los Angeles by promises of fame and fortune, and about how I got blacklisted by Cupcake and meeting Captain Bob and White Buffalo Spirit and everything looking so great and then just falling to pieces— one incredible, outrageous story upon the next.

As I talked, Kate's eyes got bigger and bigger and her mouth fell open. When I started to cry, she started to cry, and I knew she wasn't supposed to, which made me laugh, which made her laugh, and pretty soon we were howling with laughter.

When we were finally able to get up off the floor, gasping and handing each other tissues, I said, "Hey, are we supposed to be having this much fun?"

"I'm not supposed to react to anything you say, but I can't help it!" Kate said. "Everything you're telling me is so awful, but at the same time, it's totally hilarious! I can't believe the life you've led! I've never heard anything like this! No wonder you're upset!"

"So you think I am legitimately upset? Or do you think I'm crazy?"

"I think you're legitimately upset!"

This was a relief, I can tell you. I was tired of being told I was a head case. I couldn't wait to tell my zombie friends that my therapist said I had a real reason to be mad at the world.

I guess spilling my guts and actually getting some real understanding was what I needed, because Kate and I only had a few more sessions after that.

One day I asked her, "Kate, during the time you've known me and we've talked like this, have I ever given any indication that there is something wrong with me? I mean, have I ever said or done anything in front of you that made you think, uh-oh, she's a schizo?"

"Well, Evie, it doesn't really matter what I think. It only matters what you think," she said, bless her. "Do you think there is something wrong with you?"

"No, actually, I don't."

"Well, neither do I," she said.

My therapy was over.

"Well! I guess that's that then!" I said. "But look, I'd really like for us to stay friends. I really like you, Kate."

"I really like you, too, Evie!"

Because of the clinic policy or some weird rule designed to protect therapists from malpractice suits, we can't have any social contact for a while, but I'll find you, Katie!

STUPID DRUG MUSIC

It took me a while to figure out the connection, but if you look at the history of music and the history of drug culture, you can see the relationship. Popular music is always related to the popular drugs.

Think about it.

The music of the '60s was LSD music. Look at The Grateful Dead. You had to be on acid to get them. Have you tried listening to the music of The Grateful Dead in a normal state of mind? It hardly makes any sense at all!

'70s music was potheads-turning-into-coke-users music.

The music in the '80s and early |'90s was definitely coke and heroin music. Listen to old Billy Idol—you can hear that everyone involved with those records was coked out of their minds. There's barely any production. That's how coke is. There's practically nothing going on, but it is a very intense, almost apocalyptic nothingness.

I met the guy who produced those records at a studio in Hollywood one night. He was so wired he was frothing at the mouth, and was listening to the same bell sample over and over, stomping his feet like an overexcited six-year-old and yelling, "Shit! That's hot! That is fuckin' great!" like he was listening to the most slammin' rock and roll record ever.

He was listening to a *bell sample.* Ping! Ping!

Anybody who walked into the room was forced to sit at the console to listen to the bell sample with you-know-who moshing all over the place to Ping! Ping! That's what coke records are like.

Heroin records are like Guns n' Roses and Nirvana. Heroin music is all about screaming, self-hatred, and naked girls. Of course, coke music is about naked girls and screaming, too, but the hatred is directed outward, at others. Actually, that's not really hatred, but natural paranoia amplified to the nth degree, which comes across looking a lot like hatred.

Coke is like, "I know you're out to get me, so I'm going to have to kill you." Heroin, on the other hand, is more like, "I know you're all just using me, so I'm going to kill myself."

The naked girls are just a prop in both cases, but mainly with the coke bands. I guess coke makes people horny before they get paranoid and try to kill you. People on heroin don't seem all that interested in sex or killing people, I've noticed. They are mainly interested in heroin.

I was doing just fine in England when people just drank like fish and smoked hash.

But then everybody started taking Ecstasy and hanging out in large zombie touchy-feely groups in the middle of nowhere, which was called "going to a rave." ("Going to a *Rave*?") Ecstasy music is all sort of whiningly dreamy repetitive stuff that doesn't go anywhere. Ecstasy is like that. For a few hours you think you're having this wonderful dreamy, aren't we all just beautiful time. Then it wears off and you haven't done anything for hours but get felt up by a bunch of ugly slobbering loons, but you barely remember anything anyway so it doesn't matter. Try listening to "rave" music when you're not on Ecstasy. It's fucking boring! But that's what happened in England.

So when I came to California everyone was on coke and heroin or just got off coke and heroin, or was about to start doing coke and heroin. I tried both, but it caused problems with my creativity. I've said, and I read that Joni Mitchell said the same thing once, when you're on drugs, you think you're doing all these wonderful creative things, but actually all you're doing is drugs. So I quit doing drugs, and suddenly I lost all my friends and nobody wanted to work with me anymore. If I had kept doing drugs, I probably wouldn't have written all these great songs, but then, people who are on drugs don't really care about great songs, they like to hear noise that goes with the drug their on.

* * *

In the mid-'90s, I found I was screwed again because everybody who used to do drugs stopped doing drugs and joined twelve-step programs. So I still didn't have any friends because I wasn't recovering from an addiction, a problem I most certainly must have, I was told, because anybody who is anybody is a recovering addict, and anyone who says they are not an addict is in denial, and therefore is a nobody to be shunned.

At that point I became an alcoholic and started hanging around AA meetings, which turned out to be where all the truly crazy people are.

Next thing you know, the airwaves were taken over by people who look and act like they're doing drugs, but *they're* not *doing* drugs— they are *selling* drugs to people who then become their zombie fan base and buy all their records because the music goes with the drugs! Isn't that clever?

So all I have to do is just figure out which drug goes with my music, start dealing the drug, and sell records to my doped up clients…get a few bench ads…a billboard or two…and voila! I'm Puffy Combs! Or whatever his name is these days.

Okay, so what is everyone on now?

Prozac, Ritalin, and Viagra. Maybe I should start doing a whole bunch of that stuff so I can figure out what kind of noise I should be selling to the poor fucked up Americans. Palm Springs is a great place to do this kind of research, since it is full of old people on Viagra and gay people on Prozac and mentally ill people on Ritalin who have a lot of time on their hands.

But right now, I need a break. I am exhausted from trying to figure out Hollywood. I'm just going to lie by the pool and do crossword puzzles until it gets too hot.

Then maybe I'll get up, go inside, pop some of my mom's Prozac and think about writing some stupid drug music.

Nah.

OASIS

The desert is really beautiful in the springtime. The light is amazing. I like to watch the hills and mountains surrounding this valley change as the sun moves across the sky.

The view is always surprising, the landscape fascinates me. I spend a lot of time in the Thousand Palms oasis, though it would be more accurate to call it Eighty Palms, and you can't swim in the pond anymore because of the endangered pup fish, which look suspiciously like regular old guppies to me. A couple of crayfish live in there though, and I found some freshwater clams. I haven't tried to eat them yet, but I'm learning about desert plants, many of which are nutritious if not medicinal.

Aunt Jet and Hellcat moved to Texas.

Roberto kissed enough asses to win a couple of Grammy Awards.

Ferret Girl accused her boss of sexual harassment and sued him for millions, but didn't get away with it. She works in a pet store now.

The Spamalope became very successful singing commercials.

After the furor of the stalking thing died down, Reuben went back to selling houses. We don't talk anymore.

The legendary Sparky Goldstein died, and I went to his memorial service and laughed and cried with the remaining Angry Old Men, Sparky's ex-wives and children. Burt Polk was there and I thanked him for telling me the truth that day at Jerry's Deli. He didn't remember me.

I'm getting to know my mother. Former Tennessee beauty queen, talented, frustrated painter. My mother was thrilled to receive me when I came out here in my broken-hearted state. I expected her to gloat, but she seems genuinely pleased to have me nearby.

She gets a little attitude, though. The first thing she said to me when I arrived was "I'm sorry, Evie, but I don't have any *champagne.*"

Sometimes I really miss Los Angeles. I don't know why. Maybe because when I lived there I was young and silly and full of hope like all the other millions of young people who flock to Hollywood every year. Everything was exciting, everyone was fabulous. Every so often the blather and gab and networking and favors pay off and something happens, somebody sleeps with the right person and actually gets a record out, or somebody makes a film.

I think what created the sense of excitement was the feeling that great things were always *almost* happening. Great things *almost* happened for me, too. It was fun. It was painful and crazy and utterly ridiculous, too, of course.

People call from L.A. now and then and say they'll visit, but they never do, even though I'm only two hours away. I don't mind. They're busy.

Plus I've gotten used to living like a hermit, the silence and the space. Every now and then I get the bug to dress up and go out and people go, "Hey, aren't you that girl, um, whatsername..."

But I'm thinking about music again.

I'm even working on a new song.

It goes, "How's the air up there, on FM Radio..."

Printed in the United States
63615LVS00005B/4-9